A CAT'S CHRISTMAS

Also by Stefanie Samek:

Purring in the Light: Near-Death Experiences of Cats

A CAT'S CHRISTMAS

Stefanie Samek

Illustrations by Larry Ross

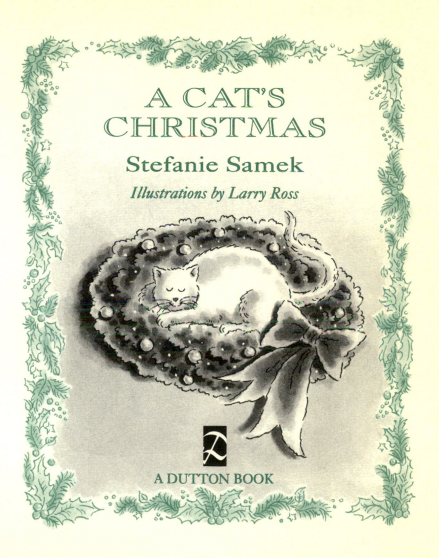

A DUTTON BOOK

DUTTON
Published by the Penguin Group
Penguin Books USA Inc., 375 Hudson Street,
New York, New York 10014, U.S.A.
Penguin Books Ltd, 27 Wrights Lane,
London W8 5TZ, England
Penguin Books Australia Ltd, Ringwood,
Victoria, Australia
Penguin Books Canada Ltd, 10 Alcorn Avenue,
Toronto, Ontario, Canada M4V 3B2
Penguin Books (N.Z.) Ltd, 182–190 Wairau Road,
Auckland 10, New Zealand

Penguin Books Ltd, Registered Offices:
Harmondsworth, Middlesex, England

First published by Dutton, an imprint of Dutton Signet,
a division of Penguin Books USA Inc.
Distributed in Canada by McClelland & Stewart Inc.

First Printing, November, 1996
10   9   8   7   6   5   4   3   2   1

 REGISTERED TRADEMARK—MARCA REGISTRADA

LIBRARY OF CONGRESS CATALOGING-IN-PUBLICATION DATA

Samek, Stefanie.
    A cat's Christmas / Stefanie Samek ; illustrations by Larry Ross.
        p.   cm.
    "A Dutton book."
    ISBN 0-525-94123-1
    1. Cats—Humor.   2. Christmas—Humor.   I. Title.
    PN6231.C23S35   1996
    818'.5407—dc20   96-17304
                                                                CIP

Printed in the United States of America
Set in Century Expanded
Designed by Leonard Telesca

This book is printed on acid-free paper.

To cat lovers everywhere—but especially
Camille and Jack Groves,
who make it Christmas for their cats
every day of the year.

Contents

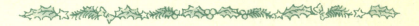

Contents

Cat Christmas Poems, Carols, and Stories

Thanks to

Deirdre Mullane, my editor, for her extraordinary vision,
shrewd judgment, and encouraging purrs.

Larry Ross, for being clever, funny, committed to
excellence, and always such a joy to work with.

Carole Abel, my agent, who is as warmhearted and genial
as she is farsighted and smart.

Richard Waldburger, my husband, for his wise counsel
and constant loving support.

Barney, Maui, Fluffy, Sheba, and Charlie, the white-mitted
Ragdoll who inspired Santa Paws.

Introduction

It is Christmas Eve in New England. A Maine Coon kitten, pink nose pressed to an icy windowpane and round golden eyes fixed on a midnight sky of swirling snow, watches for Santa Paws. On the wide wooden planks of the farmhouse floor, a saucer of milk and a dish of dry kibbles await his arrival.

Inside an adobe house in the Southwest, the air is fragrant with piñon and pine. As orange embers smolder, smoky vestiges of the fire waft around a tabby family who hang their stockings on the kiva hearth. A brown ball of fur races around his first Christmas tree, batting at chili pepper chains, brilliantly colored paper birds, corn husk cats, and tiny mice made of woven straw, causing them to flap and swing wildly on their branches.

In a Tyrolean cottage nestled in the foothills of the Alps, faint sounds of pawing and scratching intrude on the audible

silence of the winter night. A Swiss shorthair, the color of buttermilk and renowned for her delicate claw-crafts, puts finishing touches on a Christmas gift.

Before retiring for the night, a British shorthair in a London flat paws through a well-worn copy of *A Cat's Christmas Carol*, considers how lucky he is to have the central heating his Victorian ancestors lacked, and offers a little prayer up for all the homeless cats, meowing, as Tiny Tomcat once meowed, "God bless you, every one."

All over the world, cats celebrate Christmas, with customs and traditions that are uniquely theirs. Did cats always celebrate Christmas? Do domestic tiger tabbies celebrate in the same fashion as Norwegian Forest Cats, Russian Blues, or Tonkinese? Who is Santa Paws, where did Hide & Seek the Ornaments come from, and why do we celebrate the Nine Nights of Christmas? Just when did it all begin? It's a tale worth telling, and for the first time in feline history, the complete story is being told.

In a heritage that dates back to the Celtic kitties who once scratched glyphs in the rocks around Stonehenge, the masked Roman cats who paraded through the streets during Caturnalia, and those first felines to ride astride the mighty Yowl Log, it's a holiday cloaked in rich tradition. Fragments of this fascinating history still cling to the customs of today, much like red velvet cushions carrying the memory of white Persian fur.

In *A Cat's Christmas*, we'll dig into the origins of this

special holiday and trace the evolution of many time-honored cat Christmas rituals and traditions. We'll unravel several ancient myths, snuggle up with some favorite carols and Christmas stories, and get tips on everything from decorating a tree to how to extend a charitable paw to those in need. There's even a journal that allows you to preserve your own treasured memories for litters to come. *A Cat's Christmas* is also a kitten's Christmas, because it's only through them that Christmas lives on.

Now it's time to sink into a soft sofa and revel in the magical sounds, sights, and scents that are the season. Crackling

logs, tinkling bells, crinkling paper bags being emptied of their contents. Twinkling lights, whirling ornaments, shimmering tinsel, glittering papers, fluttering ribbons. Perk up your ears. Let your eyes widen with wonder and your whiskers twitch in happy anticipation as holiday platters appear piled high with festive foods, mysterious wrapped packages beg to be inspected, and open boxes invite you in.

How reassuring it is to know that Christmas has returned; the time when your family curls up a little closer, celebrates the miraculous, and shares special warmth. At the heart of it all there's love and a sense of magic. It's something every cat can sense, and at Christmas, it brightens the spirits of creatures everywhere.

Merry Christmas, and may you all find reasons to purr.

A History
of the Holiday

Christmas is a time of merriment and feasting, a time when cats indulge in all the traditional pleasures: scaling the Christmas tree, gobbling up turkey and kibbles, yowling carols, and eagerly awaiting gifts from Santa Paws. Warm fur bodies are positioned close to the hearth, relishing a long, uninterrupted snooze. Yet these cherished feline traditions weren't always with us. They evolved over time.

Back in the days when cats didn't have lamps, electric blankets, or down comforters to help them maintain an agreeable body temperature, winter was a cold, dark, and nasty time. Although our feline ancestors spent 70 percent of their lives asleep, the remaining 30 percent was spent chasing away the gloom.

To improve this bleak state of affairs and to hasten the return of the warming sun on their fur, cats created a special

winter solstice festival. As pagan as it was, this festival had all the earmarks of Christmases to come.

The earliest records of these solstice rituals were left by Celtic cats living in the British Isles. Celtic claw glyphs deeply etched into the rocks at Stonehenge detail pagan pussycat rites involving oak trees, magical and deadly mistletoe, and unbridled passion behind the stones.

Just how, you might wonder, did cats know when it was the winter solstice, the shortest day of the year? This change from short to longer days wasn't something sudden or obvious; it was incredibly subtle.

Unlike many of today's city-dwelling felines, ancient Celtic cats lived close to nature, enjoying a slow pace with set patterns. In a world unobstructed by streetlights or high-rises, changing shadows provided the architecture of the landscape. When the sun on your favorite rock shifted, you noticed.

But cats also had another way of detecting the lengthening days, a way that was more precise. Its secret is hidden in one of the greatest marvels known to Felinedom—the Catnap Mounds.

By decoding claw glyphs scratched in the rocks near Stonehenge, archeologists came upon an astonishing tunnel of hard-packed earth that served not only as a warm bunker for chilly Celtic kitties but also worked as a celestial clock—as the design for this normally dark catnap mound was calibrated to the ascension of the solstice sun.

On the dawn of the winter solstice, light from the sun would pour in through a narrow opening above the door and light the normally dark, long, and narrow passage that was filled with soundly napping cats. This sudden and dramatic illumination stirred even the heaviest sleepers out of their slumber. Feeling the rays of sunlight on their fur, cats would spring from sleep, crawl outdoors, and meow news of the solstice to all within earshot.

Claw glyphs also reveal that for these pagan, tree-worshipping felines, ritual Climbing of the Oak Trees was the traditional way to mark the date. One by one, trembling cats would ascend, scratch their mark on a branch, and descend. Rather than face humiliation in front of their tribe, even trembling scaredy-cats would choose to scale the oaks and suffer a few broken nails.

Because they believed that the poisonous mistletoe that clung to the oaks had magical powers, such as enhancing a cat's ability to see in the dark, Clawing Down the Mistletoe was the high point of the ritual and provided its dramatic, and dangerous, finale. Given the prickly nature of mistletoe, it's likely that most celebrants were well fortified with catnip before the rites even began.

Stonehenge only set the stage for solstice rituals to come. Throughout history, we find cats celebrating at the same time each year, in decidedly different ways.

Even in ancient Egypt, the solstice celebration had a feline

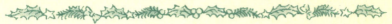

theme, since the great sun god, Ra, was nicknamed the "Great Cat." During the Egyptian festivities it was customary for cats to let out loud, piercing caterwauls in order to awaken Ra as he catnapped in the darkened winter sky.

Later, during a nine-week Roman Caturnalia, cats donned masks and marched in a purrade. Rome's Coliseum was the hopping-off point for this midwinter festival that attracted cats of every strata—mousers, shop cats, house cats, noble cats, and temple cats alike.

Happily, the Roman historian Senecat has left us with manuscripts that, although fur-covered and shredded, are still rich in vivid detail. According to Senecat's accounts, after ceremoniously washing behind their ears and scent-checking the other felines who had assembled at the stadium, Roman cats took to the streets in a high-spirited torchlight procession along the Via Gatti.

To add to the mystery and excitement, cat celebrants hid their spots and stripes behind elaborate masks, decorated with feathers, ribbons, and jewels. Masquerading felines, with their whiskers tucked well out of sight, wore the faces of dogs, mice, donkeys, birds, and pigs. In gay abandon, the procession filled the streets, going from house to house, gathering in intensity as it moved.

During the Caturnalia, the Romans opened their doors to all cats who sought entry—serving them lavish feasts of Tiber fish on shredded quail and *calamari* kibbles. Since the

Romans believed that giving presents brought good fortune, cats became the recipients of elaborate gifts. Trinkets such as tiny hand-painted mouse figurines, miniature candles with gold-leaf mouse ears and straw tails, and walnut shells decorated with bells were the most sought-after items of the day.

For nine bawdy, catnipping nights, carousing cats were encouraged to eat at the table, nap on prized togas, shred leather sandals, climb Roman shades, and treat treasured jewelry and valuable golden coins as if they were toys.

To further entertain their reveling *gatti*, the Romans decorated their villas with cats' eye-level branches of laurel, olive, myrtle, ivy, holly, and fir. Decorative garlands and wreaths of greens festooned villas, public buildings, and cobblestone curbs. Dismantling these greens and dragging them through the streets was another highlight of early Roman feline fun.

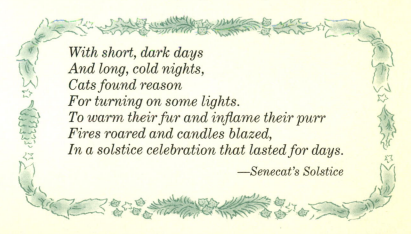

With short, dark days
And long, cold nights,
Cats found reason
For turning on some lights.
To warm their fur and inflame their purr
Fires roared and candles blazed,
In a solstice celebration that lasted for days.

—*Senecat's Solstice*

But in other locales, a bit farther north, recognition of the solstice took on a cooler tone. In northern Europe and Scandinavia, where it was believed that the Norse goddess Freyja rode through the skies in a golden chariot pulled by two felines, Swedish, Danish, and Norwegian Forest Cats customarily would feast on salmon and herring, sip bracing kitty glögg, and climb around in the pine trees before collapsing in the snow.

Since the winter solstice always coincided with some of the most brutally cold European winter nights, and there was no central heating, cats stayed in bed, trading heat with other fur-bearing friends, or curled up by a fire to vocalize, yowling out their favorite tunes.

This marked the beginning of a tradition that would keep holiday home fires burning brightly for litters to come: the Yowl Log. It all began with a simple feline observation. To keep a fire sputtering in the hearth required a huge, slow-burning log, and the bigger the log, the bigger the fire and the warmer the cat.

Tracking down the perfect Yowl Log required intensive woodland research and several laps of kitty glögg. When the right log was found, customarily, a cat would yowl with excitement; sniff the log to gauge the tree's history, health, and age; and scratch at the bark as a final mark of approval.

On solstice eve, the house with the biggest Yowl Log was always overrun by heat-seeking celebrants. As was the

custom, cats used their noses to detect the hearth with the most flamboyant blaze, and invited themselves in.

Like the Romans, the northern Europeans also believed that hosting cats brought them good luck. Whiskered guests traditionally were offered cat-size tankards of milk or kitty glögg, vessels of kitty stew, and an invitation to squeeze into the sea of purring bodies by the fire. To repay the hospitality, felines would gather in front of the blazing fire and yowl out

popular Yowltide songs, such as "Ye Brightly Burning Yowl Log," "Yowl Yowl Yowl," and "Thy Hot Fur Makes Me Purr."

But for many, the first Christmas, in all its sacred splendor, really began in Bethlehem when Jesus was born. All felines are especially fond of an old cat folktale that tells of the special role they played in that blessed event. On this holy night, many animals were keeping watch at the manger. According to the tale, when Mary gave birth to Jesus, a stable cat also was giving birth to a litter of kittens.

Later on that evening, the blessed infant was tossing fitfully in the manger, and Mary asked all the animals in the stable for help in lulling him to sleep. In their softest and sweetest voices, turtledoves cooed, lambs baaed, cows mooed, and donkeys brayed, but nothing helped. Finally, a tiny kitten found its way to the baby Jesus, curled up close beside him, and purred him to sleep.

To honor the kitten, the Almighty decided that from that day forward, only cats would be given the gift of a purr, and the sound of their purr would bring peace and joy to all those who heard it, until the end of time.

Several days later, three wise cats from the East came to visit the manger, bearing gifts of catnip, gold, frankincense, and pyrrh.

For all cats and all creatures, Christmas was truly born.

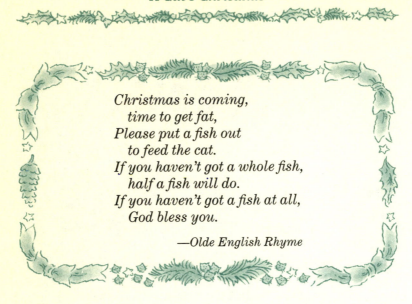

Christmas is coming,
  time to get fat,
Please put a fish out
  to feed the cat.
If you haven't got a whole fish,
  half a fish will do.
If you haven't got a fish at all,
  God bless you.

—*Olde English Rhyme*

Cat Customs Cross the Seas

When cats first immigrated to America, the Christmas traditions of their furfathers sailed with them. Although America was destined to become a feline melting pot of different breeds from all over the world, during those first holidays, cats still followed the traditions of their own kitty clans.

As time passed and the feline population grew, cats of other faiths wove their own tribal customs into the holiday tapestry. This provided cats with even more excuses to feast, rejoice, and finally snooze when the dazzling panoply of festivities reached its yearly end.

No Holiday for Puritan Pussycats

The first feline settlers missed out on the fun, for those stalwart British shorthairs who came over on the *Mayflower* and

settled in New England had the custom of not celebrating Christmas at all. December 25 was a day, just like any other day, when the hard work of mousing had to be done.

From kittenhood on, Puritan pussycats were taught that feasting and revelry were pagan practices. But many cats re-

belled. They began catching clams on the sly, cavorting in the meadows, yowling carols in the barns, and hiding under the church pews so as not to get caught. Some of these Puritan cats paid the price, ending up with their paws in the stocks and the letter *N* for *naughty* singed on their fur.

Treating the day like any other, we attended to the serious work of mousing, leaving the yowling of Christmas carols to those heathen felines whose unbridled displays of merriment invariably earned them a whack upon the tail.

—*Cottonpaws Mather,*
Confessions of a Puritan Cat

But eventually these early feline revelers got their way by creating their own holiday called Thanksgiving, devoted to catnaps and sumptuous turkey feasts.

Las Pussadas in the Southwest

For hundreds of years *los gatos*, the Spanish-American cats of America's Southwest, have enjoyed a holiday custom called

Las Pussadas, which means "the procession of cats" and is a tradition that may trace its origins back to the masquerading cats of ancient Rome. Typically, *Las Pussadas* includes hundreds of strolling and serenading cats, covers many miles, and requires several stops for tuna tortillas along the way.

Every Christmas Eve tiny luminarias (paper bags filled with votive candles set in kitty litter) are positioned along the pathways and streets to light the way for the cats and the mariachi bands that accompany them. As they pad from village to village and house to house, it's customary for cats to shred the paper-bag luminarias, blow out the candles, and scatter kitty litter to the winds for good luck.

The culmination of *Las Pussadas* is a piñata party. A brightly colored cat-shaped container is filled with treats and catnip toys. Traditionally it's hung from the low limb of a tree, and celebrants are encouraged to climb out on the limb and swat at the piñata or to feverishly bat at it from below. When the piñata finally smashes open, cats join in a snarling scramble to capture the toys and treats on the ground. As hisses mix with melodious meows and mariachi music, *Las Pussadas* comes to an end.

Midnight Feline Feasting

Still following traditions brought over from their native France, the Chartreuse and French-American shorthairs of

20

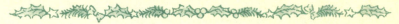

Louisiana put a Gallic spin on Christmas Eve by serving dinner late. No matter how loudly feline stomachs may rumble and hungry Chartreuse may grumble, this dinner, called *Réveillon*, isn't served until midnight. But as the clock strikes twelve, exquisite delicacies such as Alligator Tidbits, Crayfish Pâté, Oysters Felix, Crab Quiche, Shrimp and Chicken Creole, and Cajun Dogfish are served.

For dessert, there's Crème Brûlée, followed by the gala presentation of an intricately decorated cat cake, with silver whiskers and spun sugar fur, known as the Père Noel (Father Christmas) cake. This kibble-batter cake is rich in both taste and tradition. The recipe calls for nine layers, each separated by a minced fish filling. Customarily these are tuna, trout, mackerel, mullet, crayfish, clam, oyster, crab, and shrimp, layered in that order. In case of food shortages, lack of qualified fishermen in the family, or limited funds, the recipe can be adjusted to include different fillings, but without nine layers it's not a Père Noel.

French etiquette also requires that cats and kittens exercise good table manners and eat all nine layers, rather than isolating their favorite fish. Kittens who don't follow the rules are quickly picked up by the scruff of the neck and carried off to bed.

Reveillon may arrive late, but French-meowing cats all concede that it's well worth the wait.

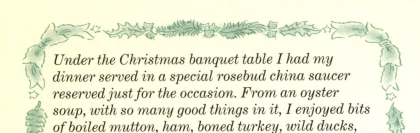

Under the Christmas banquet table I had my dinner served in a special rosebud china saucer reserved just for the occasion. From an oyster soup, with so many good things in it, I enjoyed bits of boiled mutton, ham, boned turkey, wild ducks, partridges, and, of course, oysters.

—Diary of a Dixie Cat, *1863*

The Little Kittens' Christmas

Louisa May Allcat

"Christmas won't be Christmas without any presents," grumbled Jo, giving her unusually long kitten's body a good stretch on the rug.

"It's so dreadful to be poor!" whined Meg, examining her nails, and giving her fuzzy brown and beige coat several cursory little licks.

"I don't think it's fair for some kittens to have cream, catnip, and feather beds, and other kittens, nothing at all," meowed the tiny golden tabby they called Amy.

"We've got Marmee and one another, anyhow," a sweet-faced calico named Beth chimed in from her corner perch on an earmarked pile of books. "Even though Father can't be with us for Christmas, Marmee says he loves us very much, and we should all try to be charitable and brave."

It was a comfortable old room, although the carpet and

furniture were well worn by time and tiny claws. Christmas roses bloomed in the windows, and a pleasant atmosphere of home peace pervaded it.

Noticing that the sun had shifted to an especially tattered and fur-covered corner of the sofa, the little kittens relinquished their outposts and joined together in one purring ball, as was customary at this time each day.

Jo was the first to wake in the gray dawn of Christmas morning. No stockings hung at the fireplace, and for a moment she felt disappointed. Then she noticed something protruding from under the spot where she rested her head. Slipping her paw under the pillow, she drew out a little crimson crocheted ball. She awoke Meg with a "Merry Christmas," and bade her see what was under her pillow. A green crocheted ball appeared, with a tag inscribed and scented by their mother, which made the one present very precious in all their eyes. Presently Beth and Amy woke, to rummage and find their little balls also—one pink and the other blue; and all commenced to play with them, gaily tossing them up in the air, under furniture, behind doors, and about the room, while the east grew rosy with the coming day.

"Where is Mother?" cried Meg as she and Jo ran down to thank her for their gifts and inquire about breakfast, half an hour later.

"Some poor creature came a-beggin', and your ma went straight off to help a needy family of strays. There never was

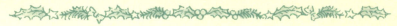

such a charitable cat as your ma!" replied Hannah, who had lived with them since they were born.

The little kittens, now hungry and eager for their mother's return, lined up by the window, eyes wide, small ears inclined outside, listening for her steps. A sudden bang of the cat door sent them all scurrying to the kitchen.

"Merry Christmas, Marmee! Thank you for our balls; we played with them and mean to every day," they cried, in chorus.

"Merry Christmas, little kittens! I'm glad you enjoyed your little gifts, but before we eat, I want to tell you about a poor family of strays not far from here. Six kittens and a cat are all huddled together to keep from freezing, for they have no fire and nothing to eat. My dear little kittens, will you give them your breakfast as a Christmas present?"

They were all unusually hungry, having waited nearly an hour, and for a minute no one spoke; but then Jo meowed impetuously, "I'm so glad you came before we put our greedy little noses to the plate!"

"May I help take things to the poor little strays?" asked Beth, eagerly.

"I shall take the cream and tuna cakes," added Amy, giving up her favorites.

Meg was already piling their kibbles into one big bowl.

"I thought you'd do it," said Marmee, fluffed out with motherly pride as she led her furry little procession out the cat door.

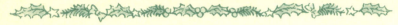

A poor, bare, miserable living quarters it was, with broken windows, no fire, a skin and bones mother, and wailing kittens, all huddled under one old quilt trying to keep warm. How their round eyes stared and whiskers turned up in smiling anticipation as the little kittens marched in!

"Cat angels have come to us!" exclaimed the mother, crying for joy.

In a few minutes it really did seem as if kind feline spirits from another realm had been at work there. Hannah, who had carried wood, made a fire, and stopped up the broken panes with old rags. Marmee gave the scrawny mother warm milk and hearty gruel, licked her face lovingly, and comforted her with promises of help while she cuddled and nurtured the tiny crying kittens as tenderly as if they had been her own.

The little kittens, in the meantime, purred words of encouragement into the poor babies' ears, cleaned their little heads, and helped them regain their strength, feeding them morsels of breakfast, like so many hungry birds.

"They're cat angels!" cried the mother once more, as her family ate and warmed their cold fur by the fire. The little kittens had never been called cat angels before, and thought it very agreeable. That was a very happy breakfast, though they didn't get any of it; and when they went away, leaving comfort behind, I think there were not in all the city four merrier kittens than the hungry little cats who gave away their breakfasts on that Christmas morning.

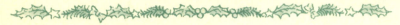

"That's loving our neighbor better than ourselves, and I like it," said Meg later that afternoon, as the little kittens and their mother snuggled together by their own warm hearth. They nestled close and, one by one, on a lullaby of purrs, Marmee and her little kittens drifted off to a sleep that was deeply content.

Cats of Other Faiths

During the holiday season, not all cats celebrate Christmas. Many continue to follow ancient pagan practices, communing with nature spirits, scratching around sacred trees, and sniffing for omens on the forest floor. Native American cats come together in sacred circles, and Sufi cats continue to whirl, contemplatively chasing their tails in a slow, ecstatic dance that is said to raise their spirits. But for many, two other holidays hold special meaning.

Cats who are members of Jewish families enjoy a seasonal celebration of lights called Hanukkat. Each night, for eight nights, a candle is lit on a special candelabra called a menorah. There are mashed kibbles pancakes stuffed with fish known as catkes, small gifts, and spinning tops called dreidels to intercept and tackle. Since it's customary to place bets on these spinning dreidels, felines have devised their own strategy to

win. Just as the betting is about to begin, cats grab a dreidel between their two front paws and adroitly dribble it out of the room.

In African-American homes, cats enjoy a holiday called Kitty Kwanzaa. The objects used in the Kwanzaa ritual are steeped in sacred tribal lore and represent the highest ideals and noblest virtues. Although most cats realize it's disrespectful, few can resist an attempt to become part of the commemorative Kwanzaa table.

Set with a straw mat, ears of corn, a ceremonial bowl of fruit and vegetables, a candle holder with seven candles, a

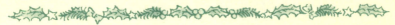

unity cup, and cherished African artifacts, the table invites feline investigation. It has become customary for cats to leap on the table when no one's watching and have a quick look around. Rather than risk being caught, any clear-thinking feline will instantly assume a regal pose and freeze, hoping to be mistaken for a piece of African sculpture.

No matter how they celebrate, cats of every spiritual persuasion find the Christmas season a time of coming together as one.

The Story of Santa Paws

Santa Paws, with his twinkling blue eyes, round, fluffy face, long and luxuriously thick silver-white coat, and enormous furry white mittens, is no ordinary cat.

The fact that he delights in wearing a Christmas costume that features a red hat, enjoys traveling in a chariot pulled by eight mitted kittens, and, without complaining, forgoes cat-naps to deliver gifts all over the world differentiates him from most felines right from the start. However, the real reason he's patron saint of a cat's Christmas isn't so obvious. It has to do with enduring qualities of spirit, along with the miraculous powers he holds in his paws.

His story reaches way back in time, and through the years, we've watched his image undergo subtle changes, like a cat shedding its fur.

Magical Mittens

According to the legend, in Asia Minor there once lived a sacred temple cat who possessed two extraordinarily large and exceptional white paws that were capable of working miracles, materializing gifts, and producing prophetic dreams.

Temple cats sought his help for everything—from territorial disputes, to scrapes, furballs, and fleas. The ancients named him Cat of the Magical Mittens, and as meows of his powers spread, cats were soon flocking to see him from all over the world.

It was said that once a year, he'd ascend into a small jewel-encrusted golden chariot that was pulled by two white Angoras and visit slumbering cats all over the East. Although Magical Mittens never revealed himself, cats were aware of his visit, for they would remember having exceptionally vivid and healing dreams that carried sacred omens for the coming year.

In addition to patting each cat on the head with his big, soft paw, Magical Mittens left a memento of his visit. Beside each sleeping cat, he'd place a little gift, such as a small embroidered silk pouch that held some culinary delicacy, or an amusing little toy.

Over time, Magical Mittens came to be known as Saint Paws, the benefactor of kittens, cats in need, and lost and wandering toms.

His Myth Moves West

When Persian, Birman, Burmese, Siamese, Korat, and Russian Blue cats migrated West, the legend of Saint Paws went with them. By the time his story reached Europe, he'd become an integral player in the Christmas pageant, moving out of the temple and into worldly life. But his saintly image didn't last forever.

In a spirited reaction to the Christmas-censoring Puritans, Saint Purr-y, as he was affectionately known, was transformed into an earthy, rakish tom known as Père or Paw Noel (Father Christmas), who was depicted with a wreath of catnip on his head and a roguish gleam in his eye.

But it wasn't until the American shorthair Clement Moorecat wrote his classic poem, "The Night Before Christmas," that Santa Paws achieved his full splendor—as a uniquely spectacular pussycat, bearing all the warm, fuzzy qualities of the Santa Paws we know and love today.

Expanded Territory

In his new incarnation, Santa Paws certainly had his paws full. Legend has it that he was now responsible for delivering Christmas presents to kittens and cats all over the world.

To deal with his dramatically expanded territory and increased workload, Santa Paws then opened a toy workshop on Santa Catalina Island in the Pacific (picked for its warm climate, favorable conditions for catnip farming, fine fishing, and proximity to the large and talented cat population in Los Angeles). He married Mrs. Paws and hired a team of kittens to convey him through the skies. The kittens were called Slippers, Sneakers, Bigfoot, Spats, White Sox, Bootsie, Gloves, and Mittens; and like Santa, each was blessed with large, white, charitable paws.

Through the Cat Door

On those first Christmas Eves, it was customary for expectant kittens to leave treats for Santa Paws along the window ledge. But with window treatments being as complex and unreliable as the weather, the plan proved unsatisfactory. The invention of the cat door offered Santa an alternate route.

Santa Paws' Stand-ins

Realizing that kittens have a hard time believing what they can't see, American felines, embracing Christmas in all its shine and tinsel, made Santa Paws more than just a symbol. They brought him to life!

Substitute Santas sporting red hats, fake-fur chin whiskers, bushy snap-on neck ruffs, and large, white furry mitts that slip over the paws became Santa Paws' "helpers." Wherever cat toys are sold, they are there—listening to kittens' Christmas lists, dispensing advice, passing out treats, and wishing everyone a "Meowy Christmas."

A Visit from Santa Paws

'Twas the night before Christmas, in the sleeping
    cats' house,
Not a feline was stirring—for even a mouse.
Cat stockings were hung by the cat door with care,
In hopes that Santa Paws soon would be there.

The kittens were snuggled in Mama Cat's bed,
With brothers and sisters curled head-to-head;
And Mama Cat on her quilt, and I on my mat,
Had just settled in to a delicious catnap,

When out in the yard there arose such a clatter
I sprang from my mat to see what was the matter.
Away to the window I flew like a flash,
Climbed up the curtains, pressed my nose to the glass.

And what in the world did my feline eyes see
But a small golden chariot, pulled by cats just like me!
With a fluffy old driver so white and so furry,
I knew in a moment it must be Saint Purr-y!

More rapid than rabbits his kitties they came,
And he yowled and meowed, calling each cat by name:
"On, Slippers! On, Sneakers! On, Bigfoot! On, Spats!
Christmas is coming! Let's go, gentle cats!

*Now, White Sox! Now, Bootsie! Let's go, Gloves
   and Mittens!
To the back porch we fly! Let's go, cats and kittens!"
So down to the cat door his kittens they flew,
With a catnip-filled chariot—and Santa Paws too!*

*And then, in a twinkling, I heard on the latch
The pawing and clawing of Santa Paws' scratch.
As I sniffed for his scent and looked all around,
Through the cat door Santa Paws came with a bound:*

*His eyes, how they sparkled! his whiskers, how
   merry!
His cheeks were like marshmallows, his pink nose
   like a cherry!
His little cat mouth was drawn up like a bow,
And the fur on his paws was as white as the snow.*

*He meowed not a word, but went straight to his work,
And filled all the stockings, then turned with a jerk.
Then washing his whiskers, ears, coat, and tail,
After having a snack, out the cat door he sailed.*

*He jumped in his chariot, to his team gave a yowl,
And away they all flew like nine cats on the prowl.
But I heard him meow, as he drove out of sight,
"Meowy Christmas to all, and to all a good night!"*

—Clement Moorecat

Santa Paws' Message

The story of Santa Paws has evolved over time. But whatever name he goes by, regardless of the length of his whiskers, size of his paws, or color of his fur, his message for Christmas remains the same. It's about caring for the needy, giving from the heart, and always being ready to share your purr.

The Nine Nights
of Christmas

As nine is the mystical number associated with all things feline, it comes as no surprise that there are not ten or twelve but nine nights of Christmas that carry special meaning for cats. Each night holds its own power and magic—and when the traditions of each night are fully honored, cats can be assured of cosmic protection, as well as meals to their liking served throughout the coming year.

The First Night

A night of beginnings. You hold the magic in your paws. Use them to investigate your house for anything that's new—presents carefully hidden away, Christmas decorations, holiday treats, or unexpected visitors—using your sense of smell

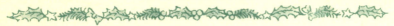

to track them down. Personalize anything you find by scratching your signature onto it. Mark the night by leaving something new in the middle of the living room rug.

The Second Night

Use your intuition tonight. Sense when someone feels tired or stressed and give him or her a friendly head rub and a healing purr. See how the Christmas tree is feeling. Lean into its branches and listen attentively. Take psychic inventory of everything and everyone in your house.

The Third Night

A paws-on night devoted to holiday decorating. Beautify your house by spreading greens around—seeing that sprigs find their way into every room. Roll ornaments into the corners. Leave ribbon and wrapping-paper samples all over the floor so that final selections can be made easily.

The Fourth Night

Boxing night. The evening to immerse yourself in gift wrapping. The moment to dust off the insides of gift boxes—using

your body, soul, and whiskers. A time to test the strength of wrapping paper and the elasticity of ribbon, while serving as a Scotch Tape dispenser with a few strips stuck to your tail.

The Fifth Night

Enjoy the ancient ritual of Christmas carowling with the other neighborhood cats. Treat the people on your street to some holiday favorites, and if your cat chorale is really in

voice, they may honor your virtuosity with a plate of Christmas delights.

The Sixth Night

On this night, it's traditional for cats to express their affection. You may choose to be selective, curling up by the fire with a special furry friend; or you might decide to throw a party and invite all the neighborhood cats to an open kitchen or back-porch soiree. This is the night when it's customary to revive the myth of Freyja and her flying cats, with a Scandinavian smorgasbord—which may include heaping platters of herring, sardines, tuna, mackerel, and salmon.

The Seventh Night

Use this night to see that all the Christmas preparations are completed to your satisfaction in your home—or, if you're an outdoor cat, in your territory. See that any greens, lights, or decorations you may have displaced in an exuberance of holiday spirit have been put back in their place. Lap up any spills, and rub your scent everywhere that needs refreshing.

The Eighth Night

A night to regain your inner harmony and make sure you'll merit a visit from Santa Paws. Devote the evening to rest, kind thoughts for cats less fortunate than yourself, and silent vigil. Enjoy some stretching exercises, head-to-toe purrs, a purifying snooze by the fire, and a series of deep-cleansing baths.

The Ninth Night

On this night, be patient and be of help to others. Make sure everything's positioned in the right spot by walking on all the presents under the tree. Place last-minute bets about what's in each box. See that milk and kibbles are left by the cat door or window. Spend the remainder of the night waiting for Santa Paws, until the magic dusting of an Angelcat lulls you to sleep.

. . . The snow-white kitten looked up at the towering evergreen tree and asked, "O wise tree, how can I meet a real prince—someone to curl up with forever and cherish?"

"Sweet furry princess, just climb up to my seventh branch and you will find your answer," the evergreen replied.

The kitten climbed and climbed. Sharp pine needles pierced her pristine white coat, and resin clung to her fur. Just as she felt she could climb no farther, she heard a long, low rumble from the branch just above. It was his purr. . . .

—*The Magic Tree, from* Grimm's Furry Tails

A Cat's Christmas Tree

Legends surrounding the origin of a cat's holiday tree are as numerous as pine needles on the rug after Christmas. Since the days when tree-worshipping Celtic cats first scaled sacred oaks to claw down the magic mistletoe, a tree has been something cats looked up to with special reverence.

During their celebration of Caturnalia, ancient Roman felines brought forth a Tree of Life, decorated with woven greens, twigs, dried figs, coins, nut shells, and carefully selected bird feathers.

Medieval kitties festooned their trees with apples, ribbons, dried herbs, bits of broken armor, magical symbols, and straw mice.

Victorian cats favored trees that blazed with the lights of real candles and were hung with decorations, such as intricate glass baubles or colorful garlands.

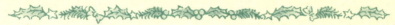

Today there's no rule of dress for a cat's Christmas tree. Beloved heirlooms, brought down from the attic; slightly tarnished silver bells; Victorian glass balls; birds carved of birch or fashioned from bright feathers; catnip-filled canes, red satin mice, strings of lights that flash, and homemade chains of nostalgia all nestle in the branches harmoniously.

Finding the Purrfect Tree

Each evergreen tree has a bright, biting fragrance that makes your whiskers twitch. Your nose would delight in a forest of firs. How do you select just one—and which one do you select?

To choose the "perfect" Christmas tree, all you need is feline intuition, allowing you to tap into the essence of each prospect—sensing its family history, how it has weathered the seasons, how many birds its branches have nested, and how it might take to being dressed up and on display. A time-honored ritual can help you make your choice. Follow these guidelines until you have identified the "perfect tree" (more a measure of personality than of looks).

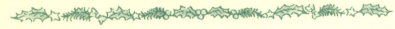

A Cat's Tree-Choosing Guide

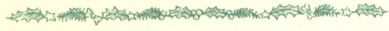

1. Sniff the tree to see if it's friendly.
2. Rub up against the branches to test the tree's health. (If it's shedding needles, move on.)
3. Race around the tree and watch its reaction to your antics. (If the tree sways in amusement, it's a good sign.)
4. Bat at some branches to check the tree's sense of playfulness.
5. Stretch out on a bough to test the tree's strength.
6. Hold onto a branch and swing back and forth like an ornament. (If the tree oozes sap onto your paws, it's unhappy.)
7. Put your paws around the lower part of the trunk and give the tree a hug. (Does it feel as though you're hugging a familiar forest friend?)
8. Gently scratch at the bark to see if the tree enjoys it.
9. Curl up under the tree and close your eyes. Use your intuition to sense how protective and loving the tree feels toward you.
10. Claw your way up the trunk and try to balance on top, like a star. (If the tree doesn't shake you off, bring it home—this tree's for you!)

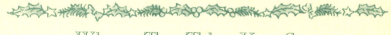

When a Tree Takes Your Spot

To cats, the placement of the Christmas tree is of prime importance. A rule of paw says it's always best if you pick the spot. You do this by circling around a location you like and meowing plaintively until the tree gets planted there. If a tree has commandeered your spot and is interfering with your daily routine, it must be moved at once.

Any tree that's sitting in a sunny spot or in a place that benefits from an entertaining vista is interfering with your quality of life and needs to be relocated. Here's what you do:

First, try body language. Give the tree a poke or a nudge. If it doesn't budge, push your whole body against its branches and shove.

When a large, bushy, overbearing tree is blocking your view of birds and passing neighborhood toms, simply rise to the occasion. Climb it. Once you're "caught" clinging to the top of a dangerously swaying tree, desperately trying to catch a glimpse of the snowy winter sky, a swift move is assured.

A tree that's too close to your spot by the fire is not only a pushy usurper of heat; it's a fire hazard. If scare tactics should fail, just grab a large branch between your teeth and, using the full force of your body weight, drag the tree down.

Fake Firs

Not all trees come from the forest. Some come from the attic. Like stuffed cat toys, they don't need water, won't shed, and last a long time.

Your first task is to jump into the fake fir's storage box and roll around in the branches. You do this to shake off any accumulated dust and infuse the tree with your scent.

After each branch gets slotted into the pole, bat at it wildly. If it flaps back and forth like a real branch blowing in a storm, act pleased. Once the whole tree has been set up, check for too much space between the branches by leaping through them. The need for adjustments should become obvious.

Use your aesthetic sense to dislodge any branches that don't please you. And then, as a final test of stability, charge at the tree to see how well it stands.

Nine Times Around the Tree

One more ceremony is required before you're ready to decorate. In order to welcome a tree, invigorate it, raise feline spirits, and attract good luck, cats perform an ancient sacred ritual called Nine Times Around the Tree, which goes like this:

Enjoy an excellent meal. Follow the meal with a short catnap, a long bath, and a good stretch.

Now stand on all fours, locate the tree, and approach it slowly and with great respect—gracefully brushing your body against the lower branches, by way of a cat curtsy or bow.

Now begin circling the tree, traveling around the trunk nine times rapidly, in a clockwise direction.

Meow at the top of your lungs. Howl. Yowl. Run just as fast as you can.

When you complete the nine circles, come to a screeching stop.

Brush up against the lower branches in a final cat curtsy.

Collapse under the tree and enjoy a long nap.

The Thrill of
Tree Trim

Having fresh pine to smell, bark to scratch, branches to ambush, and pine needles to roll around in is only the beginning. On top of it all, there's the thrill of tree trim!

Everything that goes on a Christmas tree, you observe, could have been dreamed up by you or one of your feline friends. Things swing and sway, jingle, sparkle, flutter, twinkle, glitter, and provocatively tease.

And who knows their way around a tree better than you? From top to bottom, inside and out, you're the expert. It's Christmas again! Let the games begin!

The lights go on first. You don't want them to be too big, too bright, or blinking, because they'll keep you awake. Blinking lights cause most cats to fall into an annoying wake/sleep cycle as they're apt to unconsciously synchronize themselves with the on/off pattern of the lights.

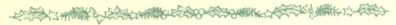

The job of hanging the lights is best left to humans. It's tedious and exposes you to dangerous electrical currents. We've all heard horror stories about cats biting wires that could make your fur stand on end—so be careful.

When the lights are up, it's your job to decide what refinements need to be made. Stand back and check the spacing. If it doesn't please you (or makes it difficult for you to navigate around the interior of the tree), try a little creative repositioning, making small adjustments as you go.

Bulb Bowling

Every season, discarded or burned-out Christmas tree lights are used for the cat game that traditionally kicks off the holiday season: Bulb Bowling.

Customarily, a coiled-up extension cord is used as a goal, and bulbs are bowled into its center—one, two, or more at a time, depending on skill. Bulbs also can be bowled from a great distance. Extremely advanced Bulb Bowlers score by batting a bulb across an entire room—or from a different room.

A meow to the wise: Bulb Bowling isn't for kittens. Keep them away from lights, plugs, extension cords, hooks, and delicate ornaments; attempt to distract them with toys of their own.

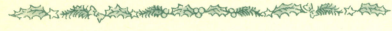

A Tail of Garlands

Wreck the halls and rejoice! It's time for the Ritual of Garlands. Garlands are long ropes—of greenery, popcorn, beads, or paper chains—that extend your enjoyment of Christmas by several feet.

Before any garland goes on the tree, take it in your teeth,

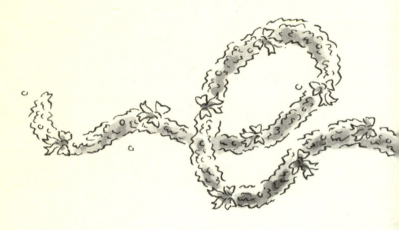

wind it around your tail, and ceremoniously drag it through the house, leaving complimentary sprigs of holly and pine-cones, pine needles, or popcorn and beads in your wake.

Try draping it in different places—under the kitchen chairs, around the piano legs, and across the TV. Parade by the sports fans in the den to see if anybody notices. Wear your garland out on the street. If you tire of decorating, elevate your holiday spirits by wrapping yourself up in a garland for effect. Whirl in circles, until you're completely enmeshed, and then claw your way out. This ancient ritual is an excellent and reliable way to test a garland's strength.

When you're satisfied, wrap your garland around the tree and take a final bough.

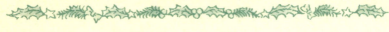

Under the Skirt

If your tree is anchored to an unsightly metal stand, it needs a skirt, which does double duty, hiding the stand and concealing you. Once hidden, you're all set to play a host of familiar Christmas games: Ambush from Under the Skirt, Hide the Catnip Mouse, Now You See Me Now You Don't, Hide & Seek, and Attack Paw.

Between games, the skirt provides an excellent holiday hideaway for undisturbed naps. You can sleep on it or under it, drag it around the tree, or use it as a tent.

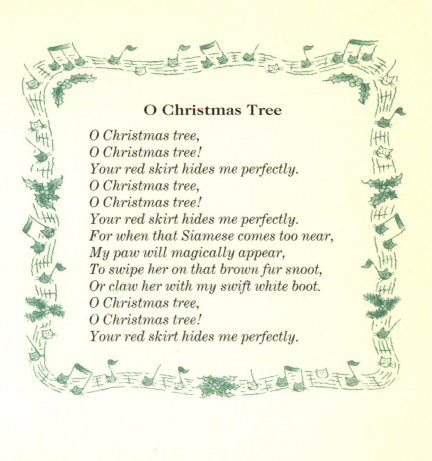

O Christmas Tree

O Christmas tree,
O Christmas tree!
Your red skirt hides me perfectly.
O Christmas tree,
O Christmas tree!
Your red skirt hides me perfectly.
For when that Siamese comes too near,
My paw will magically appear,
To swipe her on that brown fur snoot,
Or claw her with my swift white boot.
O Christmas tree,
O Christmas tree!
Your red skirt hides me perfectly.

Feline Theme Trees

As the doyenne of Christmas traditions, Martha Stewcat, is quick to remind you: "Decorating the tree to reflect feline sensibilities, feline interests, and feline tastes should be every cat's objective. If your ornaments don't have C-A-T written all over them, toss them O-U-T.

"Hide those trite candy canes, tasteless brass reindeer, and tacky miniature musical instruments under the rug!" Martha admonishes.

Here are some cat theme trees you might enjoy.

Tree of Treats

Want a tree that looks good enough to eat? With edible ornaments, you can feast your eyes and then feast your tummy.

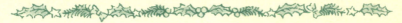

Fill bright swatches of fabric with kitty treats, twist them into pouches, tie, and hang! Tuck dry food into tiny containers or socks. Or make a long decorative garland of kibbles—mixing varieties and shapes. Cats who enjoy being creative in the kitchen will want to make their own ornaments.

Crinkle Tree

This tree will sound as good as it looks! Use materials that crinkle, crumple, snap, and crack—such as cellophane, foil, and paper bags. Rip them into fun shapes. Roll them into balls. Attach bells. Take tiny paper bags and fill them with sand. Tie them up with red ribbons and hang. They're sure to delight your ears!

Catnip Tree

This theme has all the ingredients for a sensational tree-trimming party! Invite every cat in the neighborhood and have each bring a catnip ornament! Whether you decide to do a focused theme, such as catnip mice, or a more general expression of the herb is up to you. From fresh sprigs of catnip tied up with gold pipe cleaners and bright ribbon, to catnip-stuffed socks, to catnip-infused balls of

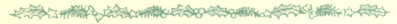

yarn—the possibilities for creativity and reckless abandon go on and on.

Fur Tree

What to do with all the fur that ends up in the grooming comb? Fur ornament balls are easy to make. Just wad up a ball of your own fur and stuff it into a piece of fine netting, sheer organza, or delicate lace. Gather the ends together, twist, tie with a satin ribbon, and hang. Recycled fur is personal, naturally scented, and politically correct!

Swatting Tree

Imagine a giant evergreen Kitty Tease. The Swatting Tree is a Christmas tree that plays games with you. Start by cutting varied lengths from different balls of yarn, from three to several inches in length. Tie them together with bright ribbons, decorate with small bells or bunches of string, and hang. Any material can be used to create long weeping-willow wisps to swat at every time you pass by. Feathers are also wonderful, with peacock the most entertaining of all.

You can even make special Ring Toys for your tree. Simply cut away the middle of a plastic lid, tie long fabric strips around the lid, tie a string around one end, and hang.

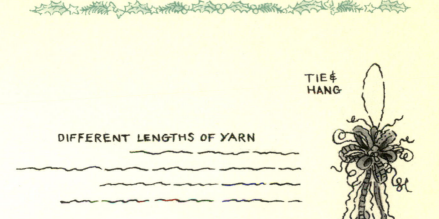

DIFFERENT LENGTHS OF YARN

RIBBONS

TIE & HANG

Cat Ornaments

Fortunately, cats are currently enjoying a resurgence of artistic adoration not seen since ancient Egypt. This makes finding feline effigies for your theme tree relatively easy. Being original takes more work.

Thai One On

If you're Siamese, Burmese, Tonkinese, or a Japanese Bobtail, play with an Oriental theme that features small china cats from the Far East, exquisitely hand-carved and painted wooden felines from Thailand, and artfully embroidered, sequined silk cats from China—with a flight of origami birds from Japan tossed in for effect.

The Cat Goddess

An Egyptian Mau, Abyssinian, or Sphinx will be right at home with a Christmas tree that's covered with small amulets of the ancient Egyptian cat goddess, Bastet. You also can mount photos of Bastet on grainy paper that looks like papyrus and hang them on silver cords.

A Tree of Stars

Here's one for celebrity lovers. Find pictures of all your feline idols—Garfield, Morris, Felix, Fritz, Milo, and Sylvester—glue them on stiff paper, punch in a hole, thread a ribbon, and hang. If you're proud of your own cat family, use their photos to make them the stars of your tree.

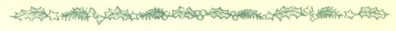

A Classic Tree

If you're traditional, decorate your tree with Santa Paws ornaments. Add shiny balls, bells, and red bows! Or trim your tree with cat angels, gossamer silk bows, tiny cardboard clouds covered in silver glitter, and macramé stars. Create your own cat angels by using photos of your cat family or pictures from your favorite cat magazines. Glue the cats onto heavy cardboard, then cut out two wings and paste them on.

Jingle Bells

Jingle bells,
Jingle bells,
Jingle on the door,
Oh what fun it is to hear
Them crashing to the floor!

Bells fly everywhere,
Ringing as they roll,
In our game of Bat-the-Bells,
Around the house we bowl!

Bells roll under chairs,
Bells spin under beds,
The joyous Christmas sound they make
Fills our furry heads!

Under the Catnip and Mistletoe

Besides encouraging seasonal abandon, decorative sprigs of Christmas greenery also encourage seasonal sport. Wherever they're hung, holiday greens are meant to be climbed, rearranged, sniffed, clawed at, and, in some instances, chewed.

Chewing of the Grasses

A fondness for nibbling on greenery is encoded in feline genes. The first wild cats who roamed the savannas enjoyed wild grasses, and today's cats relish grazing on houseplants as well as the lawn. Every Christmas, ritual Chewing of the Grasses is practiced as an antidote to holiday overindulging. Small piles of undigested grass are left to mark the event.

Under the Mistletoe

The most famous Christmas green is mistletoe, with its curative but also deadly reputation. Pagan pussycats believed this prickly green plant could heal the sick, ward off meddlesome spirits, and steer the right tom your way. (Although even the most primitive cats instinctively knew not to eat it!)

A version of this sacred ritual, called Bringing Down the Mistletoe, is still played out in homes across America. Once the mistletoe is on the floor, it's customary for two cats to touch noses and then reenact the courtship ceremonies of their furfathers and -mothers.

Mistletoe also can be carried off to different corners of the house and used for parlor games or divination. (Wonder Where the Mistletoe Went? and How Long Will It Take Until They Vacuum Under the Sofa? are two of the most popular.)

In addition, cats believe that hiding leaves of mistletoe under the furniture and rugs will discourage fleas.

Catnipping at Christmas

Although many cats turn up their whiskers at all mood-altering substances, catnip is still the feline herb of choice. Especially at Christmas.

Conscientious hosts will sprinkle catnip on the welcome mat and invite visitors to roll in it—for instant Yowltide cheer. Those who love a party atmosphere will make every nook and cranny of the house feel festive by sprinkling catnip about liberally.

If you're handy with your claws, you can create your own Catnip Rosettes easily. For the best results, use catnip plants straight from the garden. Combine them with grasses, twigs, feathers, bells, and small shiny ornaments, and then tie them together artfully.

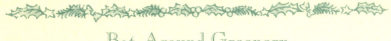

Bat-Around Greenery

Greens are meant to amuse you. Those tortured floral arrangements, with their gilded pinecones, frozen bows, and dead flowers, only sit on the mantel and collect flying fur. Gather up a fresh bunch and bat them around the house. Go for movement and surprise!

Put evergreens in unexpected places. A pinecone that pokes out from a sofa cushion, an ivy topiary lying in the kitchen sink, a pawful of holly on the bathroom floor, or a holiday swag of dried roses left on the living room sofa are all fresh takes on old traditions.

Cat Bed Wreaths

When the first Christmas wreath was being fashioned (a symbol for everlasting life, wholeness, and the cyclical nature of things), a cat promptly hopped into its center and fell asleep. The first wreaths never saw the surface of a wall but became cat beds, with twig, straw, or scratchy sackcloth centers.

Today you'll find wreaths made of rosemary, holly, ivy, spruce, hemlock, balsam, yew, and pine branches, as well as mistletoe and bay and laurel leaves. On the floor, especially with a soft, pink cashmere sweater dragged into the center, they still make a nice bed.

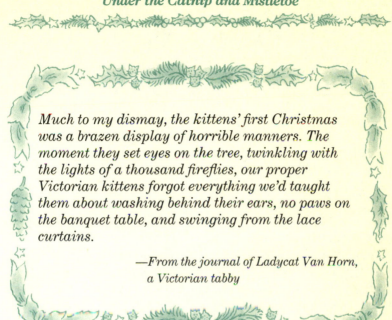

Much to my dismay, the kittens' first Christmas was a brazen display of horrible manners. The moment they set eyes on the tree, twinkling with the lights of a thousand fireflies, our proper Victorian kittens forgot everything we'd taught them about washing behind their ears, no paws on the banquet table, and swinging from the lace curtains.

—From the journal of Ladycat Van Horn, a Victorian tabby

Treat the Kittens

In addition to the festivities at home, cats and their kittens can enjoy a wide variety of special Christmas treats. Whether it's touching noses with Santa Paws or lapping up creamy catnog at a winter carnival, cat family outings bring cats of every stripe together in celebration—and hold the magic that puts the sparkle in every kitten's eyes.

The Kittens Visit Grandma

These days it's common for kittens to wonder about their lineage, with so many extended families and adopted siblings. A Christmas visit to Grandmother is a good way to show the kittens the origin of their spots and stripes, and expose them to stories of how Grandpa was a felineizing rogue.

One caveat: Don't be dismayed if Grandma doesn't recognize you and the grandkittens at first. After seven litters, keeping all those names and tails straight is no easy task.

Bell Ringers

Before you take the kittens to a bell ringers' concert, prepare yourself! The way these musical cats ring out Christmas melodies by rolling and batting around different sizes and types of bells makes bell ringing look easy. But don't be misled. Bell ringing actually requires sensitive paw-play, highly trained ears, and the ability to exercise restraint. And speaking of restraint, your biggest challenge will be to keep the kittens from joining the bell ringers down on the floor.

Beautiful Mews-ic

On stoops, porches, and rooftops across the land, the yowling of cat carolers can be heard. Why not scoot the kittens out the cat door and join in? Going from house to house, yowling carols for a second supper or tasty snack, is a grand feline tradition. Being able to meow in key isn't even necessary, because caroling never sounds like caterwauling when the voices of pussycats blend.

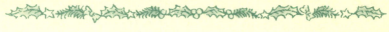

The Kittens Visit Santa Paws

Although most kittens thrill at the chance to rub up against Santa Paws in a mall, nothing delights them more than an actual visit to Santa Paws' headquarters. Preferring a hotter climate, Santa Paws and his furry flock have made Santa Catalina, an island off the coast of southern California, their site.

If you're planning to visit before Christmas, you can forgo the usual motel porch or lobby accommodations and opt for a more casual vacation with the kittens by sleeping on the beach. Santa Paws' village complex sits right by the ocean and has many tide pools on the grounds—making it easy for you to scoop up fresh seafood meals. And with sand in abundance, there's no waiting to use the facilities.

At Santa Catalina, an energetic mix of domestic shorthairs, longhairs, Orientals, and exotics, picked for their outgoing natures, friendly purrs, and ability to meow in many tongues, serve as Santa Paws' staff. Sporting red and green collars that jingle with tiny silver bells, they act as accommodating hosts for the many cat families who visit throughout the year.

Due to demand, Santa Paws has three workshops dedicated to the creation of catnip mice—claw-crafted in every style, size, and degree of potency. Another workshop, which literally drones with activity, fashions feline nesting spots known as Kitty Kozies. To keep the workers in good spirits,

Santa Paws encourages them to enjoy frequent catnaps in the nests; hence, the constant buzz.

Mrs. Paws, who's a sweet-faced, silver-blue longhair, oversees Santa's catnip herb garden and makes recommendations about how much catnip the workers should stuff in each mouse.

For the kittens, there are catnip-filled souvenirs, rides on the Magic Mouse, pictures with Santa, and memories they'll treasure all life long.

When a Kitten Asks: "Is There Really a Santa Paws?"

One Christmas, it's bound to happen. Some older, doubting tom will appear on your doorstep, and he'll begin filling your litter's trusting little minds with misgivings about the actual existence of Santa Paws.

How should a parent respond? The following letter was received many years ago by the esteemed *Cat Times*. The editor's reply is now a classic.

Dear Snuggles,
. . . Not believe in Santa Paws! You might as well not believe in fireflies, dust fairies, or the shadowy figures of angelcats that float on your wall.

Dear Editor,

I am a 3-month-old tiger tabby. Some of my littermates say there is no Santa Paws. My mom says, "If you see it in the Cat Times, it's so." Please tell me the truth, is there a Santa Paws?

Snuggles

You might decide to stay up all night to watch the cat door on Christmas Eve, to try to catch Santa Paws, but even if you saw him crawl in, what would that prove? How would you know he was the real Santa Paws and not some big-pawed, furry-faced imposter?

Just because cats can't actually see, smell, or rub noses with Santa Paws doesn't mean there is no Santa Paws.

81

Sometimes the most real things in the world are those that even cats can't actually see.

Did you ever see mice marching on the lawn in military uniforms? Or robins with shiny purple beaks? Of course not, but that's no proof they're not there. No cat can begin to conceive of all the wonders there are in the world that are unseeable and remain unseen.

No Santa Paws! Not on your nine lives, Snuggles! Santa Paws lives, and he lives forever, in the hearts of kittens everywhere. Nine thousand cat lives from now, Snuggles, no, nine times nine thousand cat lives from now, Santa Paws will continue to make glad the heart of kittenhood.

—R. Tuffy O'Fluffy
Cat Times *Editor in Chief*

I can never remember whether it snowed for ten days and ten nights when I was five or whether it snowed for five days and five nights when I was ten; or whether the ice cracked and the flustered squirrel vanished through a white trapdoor on that same Christmas Day that a partridge bone finished old Mr. Puffin and we climbed the seaward hill, looking down at fish-frozen waves, my whiskers solid-ice-sticking-together like warthog tusks, and Bessie with the kink-in-her-tail meowing why don't we come in by the fire, and we hissed and continued to scamper through the deep drifts, and my nose was blue from icy crystals and the tips of my ears cold-hard like bone china, when I finally curled crying in front of the fire, my fur drip-drop-dripped onto the pillow turning it into a sopping rag, so wet I licked myself for twenty minutes and then had a warm saucer of milk, wondering if someone will think my huge deep pawprints in the snow were left by a lion.

—*From* A Cat's Christmas in Wales *by Dylan Thomcat*

The
Season's Greetings

The first feline holiday greetings were exchanged long be-fore there was a Christmas. Back in the pagan days, nature-worshipping felines scent-marked the trees, by way of a solstice greeting, while they were making the holiday rounds. By Victorian times, paper greeting cards were all the rage. Even the most proper of Victorian pussycats became adept at clawing or scent-signing the family Christ-mas card.

As cards became more sophisticated, so did feline sign-ing techniques. By the turn of the century, cats were paw-printing, scent-marking with different body parts, licking cards and envelopes, and enclosing small symbolic trophies, in addition to scratching in prestigious cat family crests.

Over time, cats themselves began to symbolize Christmas.

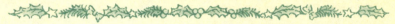

Today they rival reindeer as a Christmas icon, appearing on everything from greeting cards to tree skirts, ornaments and wraps. Although cat Christmas cards are easy to purchase, there's still nothing quite as personal as creating your own. Christmas is the season to show your skills. Cats who are clever with their claws, good with their paws, or experts at painting with their tails can put their talents to use. Here are some ideas.

Cards to Hang from the Tree

Cut out an appealing image (such as a cat, favorite food, or person) and paste it onto heavy paper that's been folded in half, placing the top of the image near the fold. Cut around the image and through the two layers of paper. Poke a small hole a little below the fold, and insert a ribbon, string, or pipe cleaner to hang.

A Photo Collage of the Family

Cut out small photos of your loved ones. Paste them together in a collage. Scratch a friendly greeting on the bottom, such as: "Merry Christmas from my furry family to yours." Make copies and mail them to everyone you know.

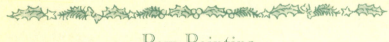

Paw-Painting

Here's a technique that's especially fun in a multikitten house-hold. Let each kitten dip its paws into washable paint and pad their Christmas greetings onto a roll of toilet paper. Encourage them all to experiment with different colors and use as many rolls as they like. You'll find their creativity has no end! Stuff small colorful wads of their work into envelopes and mail.

Environmentally Correct Cat Greetings

To make your friends more aware of the sacredness of the earth, why not send them some? Simply dig up a small portion of your own backyard and place it in envelopes. Scratch "I dig Mother Earth" on the back of each. For a touch of suspense, leave off your name so that feline recipients will have the fun of sniffing out the correct return address.

Purrsonalized Santa Paws

Ask someone to draw you a picture of Santa Paws, or find one that you like and make a copy. Find a small photo of yourself. White-out or cut out Santa Paws' face and paste your own face there, so it looks as if you're wearing Santa's red hat. Scratch "Meowy Christmas" on it, make copies, and send.

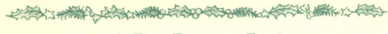

A Rip-Roaring Card

Are you the cat who cares enough to shred the very best? Then take a square of paper and scratch "Have a rip-roaring Christmas" in the center, leaving extra-wide margins of at least four or more inches around the message. Dig into the margins with your nails, clawing big gaping holes or small rips into the borders or delicately shredding the edges into long tattered strips. Paw-print your signature. Christmas is claws for celebration—so enjoy!

Send a Scent

While human Christmas cards focus on visual appeal, cat cards can easily take advantage of the other senses too. To send mouth-watering greetings, spread a soupçon of your favorite food onto a card and scratch in "Have a Most Delicious Holiday."

For elegant feline understatement, cut out the silhouette of a cat from red, green, or gold paper, mark it with your own scent, and mail, without signing. Or, to send an intoxicating message, scratch "Cheers!" and your signature onto small gold cards and toss a smattering of catnip into each envelope.

Holiday Form Letters

Too busy to pause for a catnap? Blessed with more good news than you can fit onto a card? Have more friends than anyone needs and find yourself cursed with no time to write each one? If this is your family, then the Holiday Form Letter is for you. Just pack every minute detail of your life into one letter, make lots of copies, enclose a family photo, and you're done! Here's an example.

Dearest Feline Friends,
Christmas already? Last summer spoiled us with so much
sunshine; the fur on our fortunate backs barely had time to
cool before the hustle and bustle of the holiday season was

*upon us. And here it is, time for our annual holiday letter.
All we can say is just how incredibly lucky can a cat
family be?*

*I'll start with news about me. My family tells me that
my coat is looking _____ than ever, and I'm down to
_____ pounds on the scale! The vet said, "It's hard
to believe you've had _____ litters. You still look like a
kitten!"*

*And speaking of kittens, you won't believe how they've
grown! Our oldest female, _____ , recently distinguished
herself in a local cat show by winning a ribbon for _____ ,
and has all the local toms meowing outside her window.*

*The _____ younger girls, _____ , _____ , and _____ ,
spend their days chasing butterflies and ambushing paper
bags. More carefree kittens you've never seen!*

*We're also thrilled to tell you that the boys, _____ ,
_____ , _____ , _____ , and _____ , have made us proud
grandparents once again! Between them, they must have
sired at least _____ kittens! We try to visit all the little
ones, who are now living in wonderful homes.*

*Our oldest tom, _____ , is making us especially proud.
He has a mousing job at _____ and is working his way up
the corporate ladder. With his glossy coat and confident
swagger, he continues to have all the ladies in a swoon.*

*As some of you know, we almost lost _____ to _____
this year. I can't tell you the torment I endured, waiting*

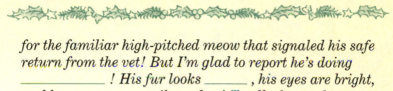

*for the familiar high-pitched meow that signaled his safe
return from the vet! But I'm glad to report he's doing
_____ ! His fur looks _____ , his eyes are bright,
and he runs _____ miles a day! To all of you who sent
cards and catnip, many thanks!*

    *Yesterday we climbed our family Christmas tree.
Seeing the decorations brought back such fond memories.
As we gather around the Yowl Log, we'll think of you and
your families, sending you our warmest purrs.*

Meowy Christmas from _____

Christmas Wish List

An empty box to call my own,
    Toddlers who leave my tail alone.
Presents destined for my plate,
    Catnip and eggnog to celebrate.
All the ribbons used for wraps,
    A do-not-disturb sign for my naps.
Trimmings to play with, satin or lace,
    Ticklings about my ruff and face.
Laps that fold out into beds,
    Visions of Santa in small, furry heads.
Fires in front of which to curl,
    Gifts that flap and whirl and twirl.
Smells of turkey, snow, and pine,
    More occasions for me to dine.
Kittens, unsullied by catnip toys,
    Ears that survive holiday noise.
More respect for My Own Special Chair,
    Fewer complaints about a little cat hair.
"A Merry Christmas" from all those I greet,
    Guests who leave the litter box neat.

Dropping Hints

Although kitty vitamins and dematting combs may be things you need, they're probably not the gifts you truly crave. Receiving the presents you really want takes feline ingenuity and requires that you start sending out loud, clear signals as soon as the last Christmas has come to an end.

Body Language

Your feline body endows you with the ability to express a full range of desires without uttering a single meow. Use it! When the Christmas catalogs start to arrive, stretch out on them and get a feel for what's inside. When you discover something you like, convey it emphatically. Sniff the photo, lay your paw on it, look up lovingly, and purr.

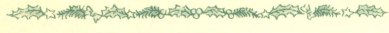

The Poor-Me Approach

Have your cat toys seen better days? Try sprawling out on top of the Cat Toys Are Me catalog and looking forlorn. As a last resort, drag all your scruffy toy mice and disreputable, chewed-up catnip balls to a central and obvious part of the house and refuse to play with them.

Be Giving

Is there something you're just longing to have? Give it to somebody else. If you surprise the dog with a stocking full of gourmet cat treats, or give the gerbil a case of Kitty Stew, chances are it will end up in your pile of loot.

Make Your Feelings Known

What if your catnip Vet Doll has lost its zip, and you'd like a new one? Let your feelings be known. Render it to shreds, leaving small piles of catnip Vet Doll all over the house.

And what if your Whirly Bird Cat Tease has lost its whirly bird? Simply deposit the disenfranchised bird in an obvious place and meow.

Remember, when all else fails, mental telepathy still works. There's nothing going on in the human mind that a clear, well-directed feline thought can't interrupt.

The Nine Catnaps of Christmas

For my FIRST nap at Christmas
My true love gave to me
A skirt that goes under the tree.

For my SECOND nap at Christmas
My true love gave to me
Two antique quilts
And a skirt that goes under the tree.

For my THIRD nap at Christmas
My true love gave to me
Three shag rugs,
Two antique quilts,
And a skirt that goes under the tree.

For my FOURTH nap at Christmas
My true love gave to me
Four Kitty Kozies,
Three shag rugs,
Two antique quilts,
And a skirt that goes under the tree.

For my FIFTH nap at Christmas
My true love gave to me
Five golden mats,
Four Kitty Kozies,
Three shag rugs,
Two antique quilts,
And a skirt that goes under the tree.

For my SIXTH nap at Christmas
My true love gave to me
Six chairs reclining,
Five golden mats,
Four Kitty Kozies,
Three shag rugs,
Two antique quilts,
And a skirt that goes under the tree.

For my SEVENTH nap at Christmas
My true love gave to me
Seven hammocks swaying,
Six chairs reclining,
Five golden mats,
Four Kitty Kozies,
Three shag rugs,
Two antique quilts,
And a skirt that goes under the tree.

For my EIGHTH nap at Christmas
My true love gave to me
Eight chaises lounging,
Seven hammocks swaying,
Six chairs reclining,
Five golden mats,
Four Kitty Kozies,
Three shag rugs,
Two antique quilts,
And a skirt that goes under the tree.

For my NINTH nap at Christmas
My true love gave to me
Nine feather beds,
Eight chaises lounging,
Seven hammocks swaying,
Six chairs reclining,
Five golden mats,
Four Kitty Kozies,
Three shag rugs,
Two antique quilts,
And a skirt that goes under the tree.

Christmas Cat-alog Highlights

In recent years, Christmas shopping has become an activity that's best accomplished curled up in a cozy ball, right where you live.

Sources like Neiman Marcats, Fluffingdale's, Cat Bowl Barn, J. Purr, L.L. Maine Coon, Victoria's Cat's Secret, The Museum Cats' Catalog, Cat Toys Are Me, Lillian Purrnon, and the All Ears catalogs make it easy.

Depending on how much money you care to spend, the choices are staggering. Here are some of our favorite gift ideas.

From Neiman Marcats

Palatial pussycat condo. Nine-bedroom villa upholstered in antique tapestries, French brocades, and fake furs. Sumptuously

soft sleeping sectionals are built into every room. A unique Therma-Paw Heating System allows the dweller to adjust the heat in each room with the touch of a paw. $1,999.95.

From The Cat Bowl Barn

When and how much you eat is finally up to you! A Cat's Choice is an ergonomic cat food dispenser that serves food when the cat presses its body on the handle. The more pressure, the more food. $29.95.

From L.L. Maine Coon

The perfect gift is right in front of your nose! Scratch and Swoon Strips transport you to places you can't always visit. A claw is the only tool you need to release the scent of salmon fishing in Nova Scotia, an African safari, wildlife in the woods around Moosehead Lake, or nightlife in a well-frequented feline-gathering spot in Rome. $14.95.

From Victoria's Cat's Secret

Now you can have a sleeping pouf just as satiny soft as the most luxurious negligee. Each down-filled Boudoir Bed is

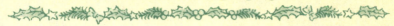

available in lace, satin, velour, or crushed velvet, and trimmed with seed pearls and woven satin bows. Specify apricot, peach, mango, tangerine, kiwi, or starfruit. $39.95.

From the Museum Cats' Catalog

For the well-bred cat, here's an authentic bone china replica of the dish that Queen Victoria used to feed her beloved companion, White Heather. The dish is decorated with tiny hand-painted chickadees and comes elegantly packaged with its own chantilly lace placemat. $49.95.

From Lillian Purrnon

Santa Paws is coming to town! This Santa rides in a golden chariot that's packed with miniature catnip toys and is pulled by eight charming white-mitted kittens with fake-fur paws. Painted on sturdy polyresin, this cat collector's item stands 6" high. $14.98.

From the All Ears Catalog

Whisker Licks *is an instrumental album, orchestrated with the sounds of food preparation (rattling paper bags, opening*

of the refrigerator, cans being opened, spooning, kibbles pour-ing, clinking dishes, etc.) and meal enjoyment (eating, lap-ping, and whisker-washing sounds). The producers claim this recording is also a subliminal appetite stimulant for finicky eaters. $15.95.

Meowing in French *is a language-immersion course for cats that will have you speaking like a Chartreuse in no time at all. Four-CD set, $25.95.*

Purrfect Presents

Possessing a keener sense of discrimination than, say, dogs, felines are notoriously hard to please. From who makes the best Flaked Shore Supper to which chair in the house offers the most comfortable place to sleep, every aspect of life is carefully sifted in the feline mind, like sand in a litter box.

Finding the purrfect Christmas present is one of the season's greatest challenges. While Aunt Honey Bun, the sedate shorthair who rarely leaves the wicker rocker on the front porch, might be ecstatic over a gift of knotted-up yarn, Lo Mein, the brainy Siamese who works in the bookstore, might find yarn a yawn.

In making your selection, first examine the purrsonality type and lifestyle of the individual who will be receiving the gift. Most cats fall into one of the following categories.

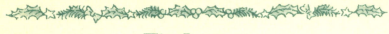

The Lounger

For a stay-at-home cat who loves to loll around the house and look out the window, consider:

A bird feeder

An aquarium

A windowsill catnip garden

The book Great Moments in Mousing

The movies Milo and Otis *and* Homeward Bound

The Tomcat About Town

For the traveling salesman who peddles his charms over a large territory, consider:

A bottle of his signature scent (invariably his own)

A catnip sachet he can present to the ladies

A customized map of the neighborhood's territorial breakdown

A gift certificate good for dinner for two on the kitchen floor of Guido's Seafood Shack

The Loving Mom

For the queen whose litter is the most important thing in her life, consider:

Donating a few hours of kitten-sitting

A coupon good for a long brushing

Commissioning an artist to paint a portrait of the kittens

A basketful of milk- and cream-based delicacies

Hiring an au purr to look after the kittens for a day

A Feline Senior Citizen

For the elderly indoor cat who leads a quiet, contemplative life, consider:

A year of "Seafood Suppers of the Month"

A basket bulging with assorted balls of yarn

An audio recording of the inspirational book Life after Nine Lives

The CD Luciano Purrvarotti Sings Italian Tabby Lullabies

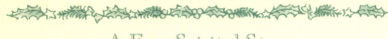

A Free-Spirited Stray

For the footloose feline who camps on civilization's doorstep only when he's hungry or it starts to rain, consider:

An L.L. Maine Coon tent

A day of grooming at the local cat spa

A gift certificate to Frisky Fried Chicken

A stray survival training course called Inward Bound

The Midnight Prowler

For the mysterious beauty who sleeps by day and stalks by night, consider:

A silver chalice for her milk

A cat collar encrusted with moonstones and pearls

An all-expenses-paid trip to sit on the Sphinx

The book The Cats Behind the Great Witches

The Food Lover

For the cat whose life is measured by the shortest distance between two meals, consider:

A trip to Alaska's fisheries

An oversized, personalized food bowl

A cat bed, shaped like a giant can of Fabulous Feast

A subscription to Gour-Mouse *magazine*

For an even more appropriate gift, consider the lineage or special markings of the recipient. Fancier breeds, and even domestic shorthairs with inflated ideas about who they are, often enjoy more exotic gifts.

For a Siamese

For these talkative, brainy cats, consider:

A language instruction course in English, Thai, or parakeet

The book Apple Heads to Egg Heads to Cone Heads: The Evolution of the Siamese

An all-expenses-paid "Temple Cats of Thailand" tour

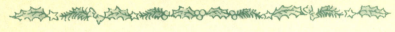

For a Maine Coon

For this adventurous Down-Easter, consider:

> *A Bar Harbor gift basket that includes Maine Seaside Supper, Clam Jamboree, and Mussels Marathon*
>
> *An L.L. Maine Coon cat bed*
>
> *A fishing weekend at Rangeley Lake*

For a Himalayan

For this elegant, captivating feline, consider:

> *A jewel-encrusted cat comb*
>
> *The book* The Katra Sutra
>
> *Fur from a cat who rubbed up against the Dalai Lama*
>
> *A gift certificate for a professional photo session*

For a British Shorthair

For this conservative, literate, and surprisingly witty cat, consider:

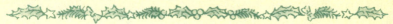

Videos of the BBC series Fluffy Turrets

A subscription to the London Times *to use for naps*

A gift certificate to Ladycliff Foxmuffin's Pussycat Parlor

A rare book, with authenticated chew marks, from the collection of Winston Churchill's cat

For an Abyssinian, Sphinx, or Egyptian Mau

For the breeds with a fondness for things ancient, consider:

A likeness of the Sphinx to rub against

A pyramid-shaped scratching post

A mummified cat toy from the Ptolemaic period

A wind-up version of the cat goddess, Bastet

A reproduction of the Rosetta Stone Scratchings

For Tiger Tabbies

For the small cat who takes pride in his or her resemblance to the big cats, consider:

Lion King *and* Born Free *videos*

A fake tiger fur throw

A cat-spotted food dish

A kitty condo with an African jungle gym

For the Kittens

To them, the whole world is a toy, so lavishing money on clever Christmas presents just doesn't pay. Safety comes first. Consider:

Sacks filled with plastic bottle caps

Balls made of heavyweight foil

A collection of paper bags

A collection of boxes

A final word about finding the purrfect presents. Cats will tell you what they want for Christmas if you observe them carefully. Where do they like to sleep? What do they like to eat? What sort of sound brings them bounding into a room and which objects inspire wild, abandoned play? Just watch—cats are dropping hints every day of the year!

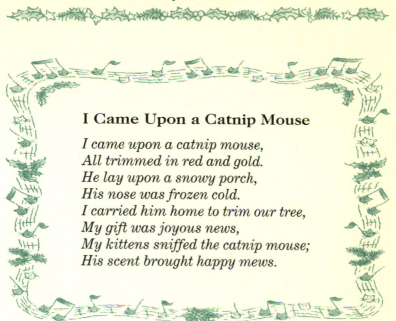

I Came Upon a Catnip Mouse

I came upon a catnip mouse,
All trimmed in red and gold.
He lay upon a snowy porch,
His nose was frozen cold.
I carried him home to trim our tree,
My gift was joyous news,
My kittens sniffed the catnip mouse;
His scent brought happy mews.

The Creative Cat

The claws that work their magic on the side of the sofa are the only tools you need to create unique Christmas gifts. Why buy it or catch it when you can sharpen your creative skills and make it yourself?

A Custom-Clawed Yowl Log

Select and decorate a Yowl Log. Scratch designs into the bark. Tie rope or ribbon around the middle and attach festive, personal touches, such as catnip sprigs, pinecones, red bows, old toys—almost anything that's lying under the furniture and looks interesting. Place the log in a spot where it will be noticed, climb aboard, and yowl. Smaller versions of the Yowl Log, made of driftwood or tree branches, make excellent feline nail files and considerate gifts.

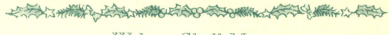

Walnut-Shell Mouse

Here's a toy you can give away or keep. To make a Walnut-Shell Mouse, use half a walnut shell for the mouse's body. Take pink felt and cut two pieces for ears and a long, thin tail. Use black felt to create two small beady eyes. Glue them all onto the shell. Make a nose by cutting out a pink felt triangle, shaping it into a small cone, and gluing it on. To create whiskers, use two short pieces of white pipe cleaner. The mouse is now complete for bat-around-the-house games. For ornamental uses, tie a ribbon around the mouse's middle and make a loop out of the end to create a hanger.

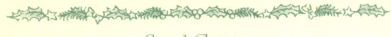

Spool Critter

Start with an empty spool of thread and a heavyweight piece of string or ribbon. Loop the string through the spool and knot, leaving a long tail. If it's going to a cat, say it's a Spool Mouse. If it's going to a dog, call it a Spool Cat.

Cat Ornament

To create this charming feline face, all you need is a shiny glass ornament, pink felt, pipe cleaners, glue, and a black marker pen. Make ears and whiskers following the same directions indicated for the Walnut-Shell Mouse. Use the marker to draw on eyes and a nose.

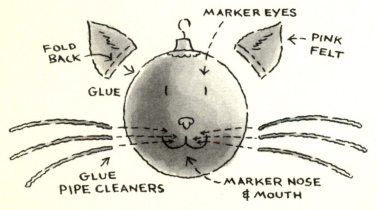

Under Wraps

Any cat can tell you, Christmas wrappings normally outclass Christmas presents. Wrappings hold promise, mystery, and the possibility of getting what you want. Open the gift and the suspense is over. It's time to jump in the box. To enfold yourself in the ritual of wrapping is to feel the Christmas spirit from the inside out.

The Ceremony of Christmas Wrapping

Box diving, tissue-paper rolling, Scotch-tape snarling, tenting under the wrapping paper, and testing yarn strength all have their place. But the Ceremony of Christmas Wrapping can be more imaginative than just whirling around in satin ribbons and racing through the house in stick-on bows. To refresh the

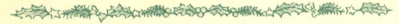

ritual, don't be boxed in by conventional thinking. Get more creative with your claws, and use your nose.

Whiskers Whipstitch, cat crafts editor of *Cat's Home Journal* and a tabby well versed with the ins and outs of gift wrapping, says: "What has been wrapped can be unwrapped. What has been tied, knotted, and delicately fashioned into dainty bows can, with a bit of feline dexterity, be rapidly undone. Experiment!"

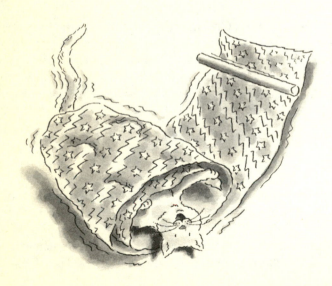

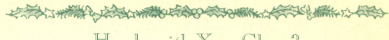

Handy with Your Claws?

Your claws can do more than scratch around in a litter box. For example:

Shred old wrapping paper into ragged, scraggly strips of varying sizes, lengths, and widths to create excelsior. Or try paw printing. Dip your paws in paint and dab the designs onto plain brown wrapping paper.

What about Claw Crafts? Shred up tissue paper to line boxes; rip out decorative stencils; or create your own free-form designs by scratching right onto wood, plastic, paper, or cloth.

Scentsational Ideas

For wonderful-smelling gifts, here are some tips.

To scent a gift box, spread a pawful of catnip or pine needles inside, and cover it with a sheet of tissue paper. To give your gift mouth-watering appeal, sprinkle some kibbles inside the box. Self-scent your presents by rubbing on them, rolling in them, licking them, and dander-infusing the contents and the wraps.

A Cat's Christmas Stocking

Some cats are born with them. Some cats are named for them. Some cats achieve ecstatic states of bliss simply by dragging them around the house. To cats, all socklike objects are meant to be stalked, slept on, fought with, wrestled into submission, and finally discarded in a dusty corner or deposited in a food dish like captured prey.

But at Christmas, these highly prized articles of human adornment take on new meaning. They're even on display! According to an old cat custom that dates way back to the pretelevision days when socks were the main source of entertainment, on Christmas every cat deserves his or her own Christmas stocking as well as somebody else's.

The first Christmas stockings were hung on the mantel in a desperate human attempt to get elaborately hand-embroidered holiday stockings, spilling over with small, enticing gifts, off the

floor and away from tiny, prying paws. However, this feeble ruse to outwit the feline failed. Cats quickly found ways to dismantle the stockings and redistribute the gifts to secret hiding places, while deriving immense satisfaction from the game.

In recent years, people have begun to hang up Christmas stockings with their cats' names stitched on them. As most felines refuse to learn to read, this friendly gesture is a waste of thread. Most cats prefer to choose their own Christmas stocking over ones selected for them.

Choosing Your Stocking is a game that requires intellect, cunning, and stealth. Historically, the ritual goes like this: While the open sock drawer or laundry hamper is unattended, you grab as many socks and stockings as you can carry in your teeth. This gives you a wide range of choices to mull over, before the big day.

Once you make your selection, you'll want to personalize it. If you're handy with your claws, you can hook your own design into the weave—pulling out long strands to knot or use for hanging.

If you want to give your stocking an outdoorsy feel, drag it with you on your next outing, making sure it picks up clumps of dirt, snags pine needles, catches leaves, and comes back well seasoned with the intoxicating smells of the woods.

For a variation on the ritual, there's the laundry. When no one's looking, pilfer several clean, warm sweat socks or knee socks right off the pile. After rolling around with them, personalizing them with your own scent and fur, you can leave them by the fireplace to be hung.

Stocking Stuffers

Once you've chosen your stocking, the next question is: What kind of stocking stuffers do you give to those you love? Since most cats are on a severely restricted budget, articles that you find or catch yourself make the most sense.

Consider surprising your human companions by returning some of the small treasures you borrowed during the year. Their lost jewelry, tie clips, buttons, credit cards, pill bottles, gloves, hair ornaments, cosmetics, and safe deposit box keys all make perfect stocking stuffers. These are the kinds of cherished items that are always warmly welcomed back. After toying with them for a year, who needs them, anyway?

Pet stocking stuffers are another matter. Though humans regard a lump of coal in a Christmas stocking as token of punishment for misbehaving, to cats it's a bat-around treat. But overall, cats prefer stocking stuffers that will stuff them, such as small bags of kibbles or cans of gourmet cat food.

In the "Just for Laughs" category, you might consider stuffing a pet pal's stocking with old corks, bottle caps, small foam balls, fake rubber spiders, balls of aluminum foil, or cut-up sponges. Since nobody remembers their stocking stuffers, anyway, don't be afraid to use the same ideas year after year.

Cat Christmas Games

Although twinkling lights and glittering ornaments, fancy wrapping paper and decorative garlands, Christmas parties and delicious things to eat help in diverting cats from the doldrums of the cold winter days, it takes even more to disperse the darkness. To brighten the season, cats have invented their own special holiday games.

Hide & Seek the Ornaments

In a diversion that's been around for as long as Christmas tree ornaments themselves, as soon as a decoration is up on the tree, you attempt to take it down. As quickly as possible, and without being seen, you quietly roll it away and hide it in a clever place. A human scores points by becoming the "seeker"

and retrieving the ornament. You score by keeping the ornament well hidden—preferably until Christmas is over. Tallying up all the hidden ornaments gives you your Hide & Seek score for that year.

Storming the Gingerbread House

In this game, a gingerbread house is turned into an imaginary castle or fort, as you attempt to take it by storm. The object is

to squeeze inside the walls, avoiding the sticky candy trim, and remain in there for as long as possible. As this game is often frowned upon, most successful ambushes are accomplished after dark.

Musical Boxes

This game was first played in olde England, during a British shorthair celebration called Boxing Day. To play, you need a recording of the tune "Three Blind Mice" and as many empty gift boxes as there are rooms in your house. A box is placed in each room. When the tune starts, the object is to dash frantically to a box and leap inside before the music stops. The object is to complete the whole circuit of boxes. If you're caught between boxes, you have to sit out the rest of the game, and it's customary to slink under the furniture and nurse your wounded pride.

Captive Laps

With the holidays, more people are at home to sit on, and many visitors (often hungry for feline attention) come by. The object of this game is to claim the lap of your choice and occupy it for as long as you can. Kneading, purring, human

hand-bathing, sweetly rolling on your back, making adorable chirping meows, and leaning your head back to invite chin scratching are all permissible ploys. The point is to immobilize the person who's "it," arrange the lap to your liking, and sleep as long as you can. Capturing a lap for over a half an hour is considered excellent.

Tiptoe Around the Trimmings

What cat can resist the temptation of a sumptuous holiday table, set with gleaming silverware and crystal and laden with steaming bowls of mashed potatoes, gravy, stuffing, and a large platter of freshly carved turkey or roast beef?

At the very moment when the guests have been seated and the Christmas meal is about to begin, a cat faces one of the greatest gaming challenges of the season: Tiptoeing Around the Trimmings. The object is to hop onto the table and make a careful inventory of the entire spread, right down to the last pat of butter, before being caught.

Ten points are awarded for every second spent on the table. Additional points are given for not breaking or spilling anything and being so graceful, humorous, and charming that you're given a delicious reward—even if you're unceremoniously dumped on the floor!

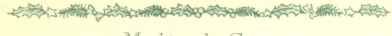

Marking the Coats

This ritual traces its roots back to early Celtic days, when visitors were rare. When strangers did appear during the solstice, cats used their cloaks to send messages to faraway felines by way of fur and scents. Today it's customary for cats to make sure that every guest's coat is personally marked before it leaves the house.

Virtuoso markers pride themselves on their special skills— turning black cashmere wraps that have casually been flung over the balustrade into white domestic shorthair coats, with deft, full-body rubs, or executing subtle rolling maneuvers that add a delicate fur lining to any wrap that's been left on the bed.

The Charitable Cat

Even if it's the last scrumptious morsel of roast turkey in your kitty dish, Christmas is the time to give it away. The generosity that begins at home often starts on your own plate. It's called being charitable, and since most cats don't like to share, it's a concept that needs some explanation.

If you're fortunate enough to be a cat with a roof over your head and a steady source of nourishment, you need to do more than purr and wash up right after you're fed. Since not all cats are so lucky, you might want to express your gratitude. You can do this by helping cats less fortunate than yourself, and Christmas is the most opportune time to start.

Feeding the Needy

Try cutting back on your catfood consumption. For every spoonful of food you consume, attempt to give one away. Indicate by

your "finickiness" your desire to eat a little less, saving the extra cans for cats in need. This simple act of charity will leave you feeling spiritually stuffed to the gills while nourishing the animal shelter of your choice!

Adopt an Orphan

Think of it—a new cat to snuggle up with on blustery nights. Someone who hasn't already heard your stories and doesn't know your tricks. A new brother or sister. Someone to give you baths, or take the blame. The streets and animal shelters are full of feline orphans who'd love to be part of your family, if you're big-hearted enough to share your nest. Extend a loving paw this Christmas and invite someone in. But remember, this is more than a sentimental gesture of goodwill; it's a long-term commitment to love.

Stray Toys for Stray Cats

How many catnip balls are rolling around under the bed? How many wind-up mice wound up in the closet? How many yarn Santas lie spent on the basement floor? If you're like most pampered pussycats, you probably have more cat toys than you need or currently can locate, and new ones are on the way.

Why not round up your old, stray toys, clean them up, and give them away to the needy?

Instead of Presents

If charity comes easily to you, this Christmas you'll have no trouble meowing "no thanks" to presents. Make it clear that the money saved on your gifts should be donated to an animal charity. You can begin with some of the national charities on this list, or paw through the phone book for a list of life-saving animal shelters near you.

American Society for the Prevention of Cruelty to Animals
(ASPCA)
424 East 92nd Street
New York, NY 10128
(212) 876-7700

Best Friends Animal Sanctuary
Kanab, Utah 84741-5001
(801) 644-2001

Doris Day Animal League
Suite 100
227 Massachusetts Avenue, NE
Washington, DC 20002
(202) 546-1761

The Fund for Animals
200 West 57th Street
New York, NY 10021
(212) 246-2096

Humane Society of the United States
2100 L Street, NW
Washington, DC 20037
(202) 452-1100

The Last Post (a retirement community for cats)
95 Belden Street
Falls Village, CT 06031
(203) 824-0831

Morris Animal Foundation
45 Inverness Drive
East Englewood, CO 80112-5480
(800) 243-2345

PETA
People for the Ethical Treatment of Animals
P.O. Box 42516
Washington, DC 20015
(301) 770-PETA

The Angelcats of Christmas

Since the very first Christmas, a heavenly host of whiskered Angelcats has been on call for the holidays. You've heard them purr from on high, sweetly mewing joyous songs. You've seen them float by your window and have mistaken them for birds. Out of the corner of your eye, you've glimpsed their shadows dancing on the walls and have felt the tickle of their tails as you drifted off to sleep. And more than likely, you've touched noses with them in your dreams.

Heavenly Advisors

At Christmas, Angelcats are always ready to offer you inspiration. Ask them a question and it will be answered.

The answer may come to you suddenly, like a bolt of light-

ning; subtly, in a message meowed by a friend; or subliminally, in a soft, ephemeral vision when you're drifting off to sleep.

Let's say you want to know what Butterscotch would like for Christmas. You're about to nap and notice you're on a red wool sweater; you overhear two cats discussing their escapades inside a knitting basket; or you have a dream you're tangled up inside a red ball of yarn. Red yarn is clearly what Butterscotch wants.

Just Meow for Miracles

Angelcats also can help you get your own Christmas wish. Speak to them directly. Meow: "Bring me a flea collar that really works." "Find me a good home." If you're deserving and always wash behind your ears, miracles can happen. Angelcats will hear the smallest mew when the seeker is sincere.

Angelic Dustings

During Christmas, cats are asked to surrender their chairs and sofas to guests, be more flexible about their meals, absorb the high-pitched squeaks and squeals of battery-operated toys, and suffer the indignities of being trapped in a coat closet during a holiday party.

With flapping wings and whirling tails and whiskers, Angelcats stir up calming currents—and with long, low rumbling purrs and a dusting of catnip, they heal frazzled feline nerves wherever they fly.

During the holidays it's also customary for Angelcats to gather on a cloud and meow songs from Purradise. Although only cats can hear them, all creatures are stirred by their sweet mews.

An Invitation
to Rub Noses

The holidays invite camaraderie among all creatures. It's a time to forgive backbiting felines, overbearing canines, and all the rude humans who interrupt your sleep. Nose to nose and whisker to whisker, it's the season to leave fur and fond memories with one and all. Why not host a Christmas party? Invite animal friends, people you love, and maybe even the vet.

How Pedigreed a Party?

Exactly what type of party animal are you? If you're a domestic shorthair who lives on a farm, your idea of entertaining may differ from that of an urban Cornish Rex. What's your style? Would you like a formal sit-down dinner, a buffet on the dining-room table, or just drinks and catnapes?

If you're the casual type, you can make the party lowdown and easy by throwing it on the living-room rug. Lay out a smorgasbord of easy-to-eat delicacies—served on top of a Christmas tablecloth or an assortment of placemats. You might even consider throwing a potluck catfood party, where guests come with a gourmet can of catfood or a baggy of dry kibbles and leave with a sampler of different treats.

Consider the menu carefully, and work toward a nice balance. Follow light seafood rolls with a heartier Kitty Stroganoff. Fresh treats, such as shrimp, lobster, and chicken strips, always disappear fast. Include a variety of wet, dry, hot, and cold foods along with some special cat, dog, and people treats.

Particularly if you're entertaining sloppy dogs, you'll want to serve tidbits that are easy to eat. The answer is paw food (such as Meow-velous Munchies or Beefy Fritters) that doesn't require utensils.

Entertaining Touches

For an amusing touch, turn a can of catfood into a kitty centerpiece. Use the round mound of food as a face, two kibbles for eyes, a wedge of cheese for the nose, thin beef strips for whiskers, and chicken cutlets, cut in triangles, for ears.

Provide your guests with separate bowls of liquid re-

freshment that are appropriate for their tastes: a heavy cream-based nog for the cats, a bone-and-brawny-bits nog for dogs, and a Caribbean rum punch with tiny umbrellas for people. Finish off the evening by passing around a bowl of first-class catnip, a plate of bones, a box of cigars, and some peppermint patties.

Easy-Does-It with Guests

There's nothing worse than a host or hostess whose fur crackles and sparks with static signs of stress. Treat yourself to a catnap and a long, leisurely licking before the party starts.

When you greet your guests at the front or cat door, welcome them with a warm purr or friendly rub. Save those third-degree sniffs for some other day.

If a guest inhales all your catnip, disappears into the bedroom with your special tom, mistakes the potbelly stove for a fire hydrant, or spills a drink on your Kitty Kozy, bite your whiskers and remind yourself that by tomorrow, they'll all be gone.

The Guest List

We invited
the Tabby sisters who live next door,
some mice who nest on the attic floor,
a turtle, two toads, a snake, and a duck,
a Dalmatian who rides in the fire truck,
a gerbil, three hamsters, two ferrets, one bat,
along with a Sphinx and an Ocicat.
A Weimaraner we met in the park
R.S.V.Peed with a happy bark.
Two Siamese who live down the street
said they'd hunt up a treat for guests to eat.
An iguana friend said he'd crawl on over,
if he could bring a house guest named Rover.
"Stop by!" we meowed to the neighborhood strays,
with hopes that they wouldn't stay on for days.
A flirtatious tom we met on the roam
said he'd come early just to see us alone.
In a nervous twitter, two robins chirped "yes";
if the cardinals are coming is any cat's guess.
When party plans were finally complete,
we curled in a ball and fell deep asleep.

—Charlotte and Emily Whiteruff

140

Favorite Feline Recipes

Christmas is a wonderful time to show off your culinary skills. Who can resist a kitchen that's redolent with the intoxicating aromas of food preparation? And cooking has another advantage: Every dish you make is one you get to taste. It's a feast without end. For cats who like to entertain, here are some recipes that never fail to please.

Chicken Liver & Bacon Catbobs

(Recipe serves 8 people, several dogs, and most of the cats on the block.)

> *12 oz. chicken livers*
> *12 oz. bacon*
> *toothpicks*
> *parsley sprigs (optional)*

Cut chicken livers into small, 1-inch pieces. Cut bacon into 2-inch strips and roll up. Thread liver and bacon rolls alternately onto toothpick skewers. Place catbobs on a rack and broil 5 to 10 minutes. Remove from the skewers and cut into smaller pieces. Garnish with parsley sprigs, if desired, and serve.

Smoked Salmon Roll-ups

For impressive cat d'oeuvres you can make in minutes, fill thin strips of smoked salmon with pâtéd canned catfood (any of the seafood flavors work nicely), roll up, and secure with a toothpick. To serve, slice into bite-size pieces and remove toothpicks.

Santa Paws' Midnight Munchies

Here's a treat to leave by the cat door for Santa Paws.

> *1 can sardines*
> *1 cup ground kibbles (crumbled in a food processor)*
> *1 egg, beaten*

Heat oven to 325° F. Mash sardines in a bowl. Add remaining ingredients and mix well. Drop ¼ teaspoonfuls of the mixture onto a lightly greased cookie sheet. Bake 7 minutes, cool, and serve. Save some for Santa!

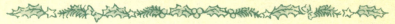

Yowl Nog

(Serves 2 cats)

> *1 egg, separated*
> *1 tablespoon sugar*
> *salt*

Beat egg yolk until it's frothy. Slowly beat in sugar. Whip until stiff egg white plus a few grains of salt. Fold it into the other ingredients. Serve in a warm bowl.

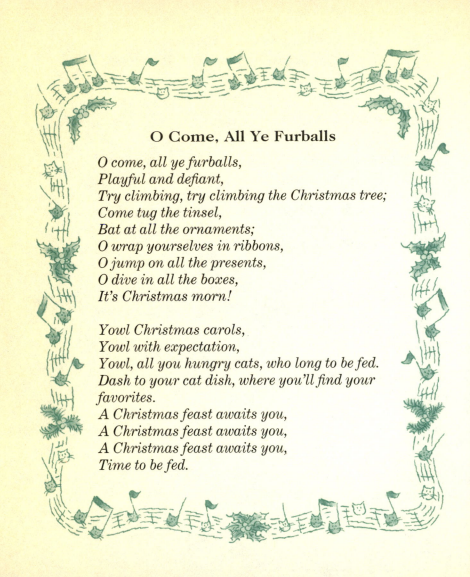

O Come, All Ye Furballs

O come, all ye furballs,
Playful and defiant,
Try climbing, try climbing the Christmas tree;
Come tug the tinsel,
Bat at all the ornaments;
O wrap yourselves in ribbons,
O jump on all the presents,
O dive in all the boxes,
It's Christmas morn!

Yowl Christmas carols,
Yowl with expectation,
Yowl, all you hungry cats, who long to be fed.
Dash to your cat dish, where you'll find your
favorites.
A Christmas feast awaits you,
A Christmas feast awaits you,
A Christmas feast awaits you,
Time to be fed.

Holiday Unwinders for Wound-up Cats

Since most cats prefer to do their catnapping, eating, and socializing according to their own internal clocks, the hustle-bustle of the holidays can be full of stress. "There's a houseful of screaming children and nowhere to run," "Strangers are sleeping in my bed," and "I feel like a wind-up mouse with a loose wire" are typical feline complaints. To calm your nerves and smooth your ruffled fur, here are some suggestions.

The Isolation Box

Locate an empty box, preferably in the back of a closet or dark corner of a room. Line it with a treasured article of clothing and hop in. Think peaceful thoughts, and chances are you'll find yourself nodding off to the sound of your own purr.

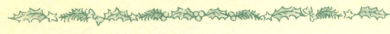

Garage Getaway

A small excursion to the garage provides a nice change of pace. Crawl under the workbench and take long, relaxing breaths. Inhale the pungent aromas of the automotive and garden supplies. Distract yourself with a thorough investigation of the bikes, barbecue, and mildewed deck furniture. If you still don't find enough privacy, you might consider camping in a neighbor's garage.

Window Shopping

When life inside your house becomes too frenetic, shift your focus to what's outside. Sit in the window and lose yourself to the passing scene. Eventually you may see something that would make a good gift or spot someone you'd enjoy meeting in the woods under a full moon.

A Christmas Walkabout

Browse the neighborhood to see who has the best outdoor decorations. If you're like most cats who have no trouble seeing in the dark, no doubt your highest marks will go to those with the fewest blinding, blinking lights.

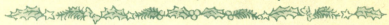

Amuse yourself by looking in on other families. If you spot a sympathetic feline friend, invite him or her out to play.

When all else fails, head for that special hideaway spot where you always find solace and where you first met Muffy. Maybe Muffy's seeking solace too.

Away at the Neighbors'

Away at the neighbors',
Tucked under a car,
The little gray Persian
Was sought near and far.
Her family, next door,
Searched every which way,
Crying "Tiger, come home—
Today's Christmas day!"

Away at the neighbors',
She awoke with a start,
The pleas of her loved ones
Went straight to her heart.
Then racing to silence
Their next plaintive call,
Tiger appeared
Meowing merrily to all.

A Working Cat's Guide to Office Parties

Today, more than at any other time in history, cats work. Whether it's dusting off the shelves in the local bookstore, inspecting fish for freshness in a seafood restaurant, or acting as the receptionist in an art studio, you and your on-the-job "family" probably will mark the holiday with some kind of office party.

During these festivities, the wise cat watches his or her tail as well as temper. At this time of year, people are prone to behave in peculiar ways, and a swipe meant in innocent self-defense has been known to cost a cat a promotion. Here are some simple rules of paw.

Sit on the Boss's Lap

Want longer meal breaks, better stretching conditions, and more naps? Then be politically incorrect. Be unabashedly

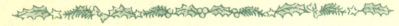

adoring to the main cat in charge. Sashay around his or her legs, purr, and hypnotize him or her with your eyes. When the boss finally takes a seat, hop in his or her lap and, while making yourself irresistibly pet-able, focus on your career advancement agenda for the upcoming year.

Maintain Your Dignity

We've all heard about Fred, the honest, hardworking tabby who was forced to have his picture taken wearing tie-on cat

reindeer antlers during an office party. Fred never lived it down. That picture not only wound up on the company bulletin board, it found its way to the "Hiss at This!" column in *Feline Forum* magazine. Don't let this happen to you!

Avoid office party humiliation by refusing to wear antlers, beaks, beards, small Santa hats, large bows, bandanna scarves, Christmas theme jewelry, or collars with tiny ornaments that blink. And never let anyone wear you like a stole!

Don't ever get dressed up, spray-painted, or decorated in anything that isn't your own fur. When you sense danger, excuse yourself and head for the litter box.

Pretend to Catnap

When the party begins to get too loud and loose, you can protect yourself from sticky hands, clumsy feet, and flying food by pretending to fall asleep. This way, no one can accuse you of lacking company spirit and leaving early. Pick your spot carefully. Never sleep where you might be sat on, spilled on, locked in, or buried under coats.

Don't Go Home with Anybody

It happens at every office party: Someone falls for the office cat and decides to take her home. Unwittingly, felines are

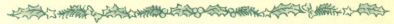

seduced with empty promises of soft beds and candlelight seafood dinners. Naive kittycats are stuffed inside lonely coworker's coats and catnapped into the night.

The next morning, you both have to crawl into work sheepishly, and the only trace of the evening that remains is some of your fur in their bed.

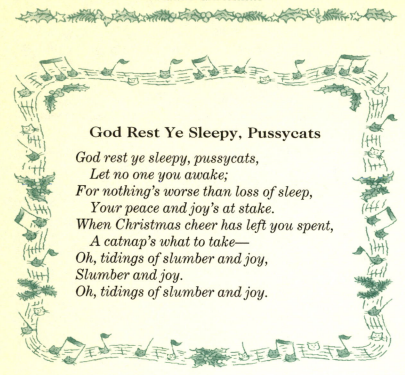

God Rest Ye Sleepy, Pussycats

God rest ye sleepy, pussycats,
*   Let no one you awake;*
For nothing's worse than loss of sleep,
*   Your peace and joy's at stake.*
When Christmas cheer has left you spent,
*   A catnap's what to take—*
Oh, tidings of slumber and joy,
Slumber and joy.
Oh, tidings of slumber and joy.

A Few Meows
About Safety

Seasoned cats know that accidents can happen around the holidays if you don't take special safety precautions. Moms need to be extra-conscientious with their rambunctious kittens. Here are some tips to make your holidays safer.

1. Make sure your Christmas tree is solidly anchored.
2. Keep any hooks out of your kittens' reach.
3. Make sure all wires are in good condition and can't be chewed.
4. Place extension cords in places where they won't be an invitation to high jump.
5. Watch the kittens around tinsel, ribbons, yarn, string, bows, or any other wrapping or decorative materials that might choke them.
6. Don't leave plastic or Styrofoam chips lying around.

7. Beware of all toxic plants that can be nibbled on (mistletoe, poinsettia, and holly berries). Keep them away from small paws.
8. Don't let guests give the kittens any food or toys that you wouldn't give them yourself.
9. See that doors that are normally open stay open and doors that are normally closed stay closed.
10. Take frequent tail counts. During the holidays, kittens have a way of disappearing.

A Cat's Christmas Carol

Charles Dickittens

Snarley was dead, to begin with. There is no doubt whatever about that. Old Snarley was as dead as a spool of thread.

Scratch never scratched out Old Snarley's signature on the oak molding next to the hole in the wall, however. There it stood, years afterward, the claw markings of both mousers dug deeply into the wood, SCRATCH and SNARLEY.

Oh! But he was a tight-pawed old tabby, that Scratch! A spitting, clawing, clenching, backbiting, covetous old hiss-face. Secretive and solitary; the cold within him froze his whiskers into hard bristles, shriveled his snout, chiseled his small ears into sharp, brittle points, and turned his fur the gray blue of soot on ice that no fire could warm.

Nobody ever bent down to pet him on the streets saying, with admiring looks, "Sweetest Scratch, how are you? Could I hold you in my arms? Would you care to come home for a

meal?" No strays ever implored him to share a morsel; no children ever inquired his name; no creature, even once, upon seeing him coming, did advance and proffer a sniff, touch of the nose, wag of the tail, or friendly rub in greeting at such a cat as Scratch.

Once upon a time upon a Christmas eve—old Scratch sat hunched over in his hall, occupied as always, busily watching a mouse hole.

It was cold, bleak, biting weather; quite dark already; and the fog came pouring in at every chink and keyhole.

"A merry Christmas, Uncle Scratch!" came a cheerful meow. It was Scratch's nephew, Tomcat Scratchit, who, with his small, struggling family, also resided in this house, and now came upon him so quickly he jumped with a start.

"Hiss!" said Scratch. "Hiss! Humbug!"

"Christmas a hiss humbug, Uncle! You don't mean that, I am sure."

"I do."

"Come! Dine with our family tomorrow in the pantry!"

"I suppose the Scratchits regard December twenty-fifth as an indolent day of catnapping and no-mousing!"

"It's only once a year, sir—a kind, forgiving, charitable, pleasant time when all creatures open their shut-up hearts freely, to be as one," he replied, backing off a bit now, tail between his legs.

"Hiss! Humbug! I say. Good afternoon!"

*   *   *

That night Scratch took his melancholy dinner of table scraps in his usual melancholy corner of the dank, dark cellar, then retired to the rotting wooden crate of mildewed table linens that he, and at one time old Snarley, used as a bed.

Now, in fact, there was nothing at all particular about the copper kettle that lay next to his crate, except for a dent that dimpled one side. Scratch had seen it, morning and night, every time he lay down to sleep and for catnaps in between. Let it also be borne in mind that Scratch had not laid one thought on Snarley since that cat's demise seven years before. Yet that night, before shutting his eyes, Scratch saw in the copper kettle, not the side of a tarnished teapot, but without it undergoing any intermediate process of change, old Snarley's face.

It was not a snarling or ferocious face, but had a dismal light about it and looked at Scratch with ghostly livid green eyes that were wide open but perfectly motionless.

As Scratch looked fixedly at this phenomenon, it was a copper kettle once again.

To say that he was not startled, or that his ears were not flattened in terror, or that his fur was not conscious of a terrible sensation to which it had been a stranger from kittenhood and which now caused it to stand on end, would be untrue.

All at once, Scratch rose himself on all fours, not caring a whisker that it was pitch dark, and began to inspect. Corners, coal bin, space under the stairs—all as they should be. No cat

behind the steamer trunks, no cat under the rocker, no cat hiding on a shelf. Cellar as usual. Old furniture, two fish baskets, mirror propped against a wall.

Quite satisfied, he climbed back in his wooden crate and crawled way underneath the linen towels, which was not his custom. But peering out through the slats of the crate his glance happened to rest upon a bell that hung by the cellar stairs. It was with great astonishment that he heard this bell begin to ring out loudly, along with every bell in the house. Head buried under his front legs, he curled tight into himself, quaking with a strange, inexplicable dread.

Next there was a clanking noise from upstairs. The noise grew much louder on the floors above; then coming down the stairs; then coming straight towards his bed.

As the Appurition passed into the cellar before his eyes, a rotting piece of wood in his crate gave way, snapping suddenly, as though it cried out, "I know him! He once slept here! Snarley's ghost!"

It was the same cat, the very same. Snarley in his matted coat, usual long pointy muzzle, usual brown spots on his yellow chin. The chain he drew was attached to a great collar fastened around his neck; it wrapped around his middle, wound around his tail, and dragged behind his body, which was transparent.

"What meow!" said Scratch, caustic and cold as ever, ears alert, feigning a swagger. "What do you want with me?"

"You don't believe in me," observed the Appurition.

"I don't," snarled Scratch. "Most likely you're an undigested bit of beef I had for supper. Hiss! Humbug, I tell you!"

At this the spirit raised a frightful screech and shook its chain with such an appalling noise that Scratch dove deeper into his crate, bringing his paws over his ears to shut out the frightful sound.

"Mercy!" he cried out from the depths of his crate. "Dreadful Appurition, why do you stalk the earth and what do you want of me?"

"If the spirit of a cat goes not forth in life, traveling far and wide, brushing up against its fellow felines, it is condemned to do so after death. In life I never roved beyond the narrow limits of our hallway, with eyes forever fixed on empty holes; and weary journeys lie before me!"

"Seven years dead. And still prowling?"

"O cat who cannot even in the darkness see! No amount of prowling now can make amends for nine lives of opportunities misused!"

"But you were good at the business of mousing, Snarley."

"Mousing wasn't my business!" cried the Appurition. "Comforting creatures was my business. Charity, cuddling, mercy, snuggling; these were all my business! I am here tonight to warn you that you have yet a chance to escape my fate."

"Oh, thank you, Snarley. What a friend! I remember how you once shared a small saucer of milk with me!"

"You will be haunted," resumed the Ghost, "by Three Spirits."

With this final proclamation, Scratch sunk under his linens, and cried like a kitten.

Then, gathering his chains about his tail, Snarley's Ghost floated out upon the air and disappeared.

When Scratch awoke from the dark depths of his crate, the hall clock tolled a deep, dull, hollow, melancholy ONE.

Lights flashed throughout the cellar. All at once Scratch's bed linens were pulled asunder, and with his fur bristling in every direction, Scratch suddenly found himself whisker to whisker with an unearthly feline.

It was like a kitten, viewed through some supernatural medium that gave it a form that was constantly changing. Its thick fur, which was of the purest white and gave off the oddest luminescence, framed great, glowing eyes that fluctuated from blue to gold to green, dissolving in and out of view like the rest of its body. Encircling its neck was a ring of catnip, summer flowers, and tiny bells.

"Are you the spirit whose coming was foretold to me?"

"I am!"

The voice was soft and gentle, almost as if it were a distant purr.

"Who are you?"

"I am the Ghost of Christmas Past. Arise and prowl with me."

They passed up through the parlor floor and out through the wall. Now they were standing in the city, where all the shops were dressed for Christmas time.

"These are but shadows of the past. No one can see us," the Ghost said.

Scratch was conscious of a thousand odors floating in the air, each one connected with a thousand thoughts and hopes and joys and cares long, long forgotten!

The Ghost stopped at a certain warehouse door and asked Scratch if he knew it.

"Know it? I was trained to be a mouser here!"

They went in. At the sight of a rotund silver tabby whose cheeks were all but obscured by a fountain of vibrissae that sprang from his jowls, Scratch cried in great excitement, "Why it's old Fuzzywhiskers! Fuzzywhiskers taught me mousing!"

Old Fuzzywhiskers disengaged his claws from the back of a settee he'd been working on and called out in a rich, jovial voice, "Meow, there! Ebenezer Scratch!"

Scratch's former self, now a young kitten, came briskly bounding in, accompanied by two or three of his own littermates.

"Yoho, my kittens!" meowed Fuzzywhiskers. "No more mousing tonight. It's Christmas Eve!"

164

With that, fuel was heaped upon the fire, and the warehouse became a snug, bright, warm room for celebration. In came a fiddler with a music book. In came Mrs. Fuzzywhiskers, one vast substantial purr. In came the three Miss Fuzzywhiskers, beaming and lovable, and rubbing up against everyone in the room. In came the six young toms whose hearts they broke. In came all the cats and kittens who lived in the warehouse, and some of their particular friends who were neighborhood strays.

There was dancing, and there was yarn rolling and more dancing, and there was chicken, and there was a great piece of Cold Roast, and there was courting, and there were fish pies, and there was catnip and plenty of cream.

During the whole of this time, Scratch's heart and soul were with his former self; he was a buoyant kitten once again.

When the clock struck eleven, the party broke up, and the Fuzzywhiskers family took their stations on either side of the door, touching noses with each cat individually as they went out, wishing him or her a Merry Christmas.

"A small matter," said the Ghost, "to make these silly felines so full of gratitude and glee."

"Small! exclaimed Scratch, now quite agitated. "Fuzzywhiskers gave all he could! With a little cream, a modest amount of catnip, a few spools of yarn, and many heartfelt purrs, the happiness he gave us was quite as great as if it cost a fortune!" He felt the Spirit's glance, and stopped.

*   *   *

Scratch awoke in his own cellar. There was no doubt about that. But it had undergone a surprising transformation. The walls and ceiling were hung with boughs of living green that invited climbing and gave the dank cavern a bright, festive air.

Just to the left of the wall of preserves, right by the steamer trunks, it was brilliant with a great light, and there in easy state stretched a cat.

"Come in! exclaimed the Ghost. "Come in and know me better, little feline! I am the Ghost of Christmas Present. Look upon me!"

With head lowered timidly, nose cautiously sniffing the ground, Scratch did as he was told, and looked.

Joyously lying in the center of a giant wreath of greens, molding his enormous frame to its circular curves, was a gigantic lion of a yellow tabby with genial face, sparkling golden eyes, and jolly manner. In one paw, he bore a glowing torch, which he raised to shed its light on Scratch as he came peeping round the corner.

"You've never seen the likes of me before, have you?" exclaimed the Spirit with a good-natured growl.

Never," said Scratch. "Spirit, conduct me where you will! Last night I went forth and learned a lesson, and if you have more to teach me, I am ready to go."

"Grab tight to my tail!"

Scratch did as he was told and held it fast.

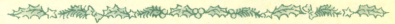

Scratch and the Ghost passed on, invisible, straight to the upstairs pantry, where his nephew, Tomcat Scratchit, and his family made their humble quarters.

Mother Scratchit, still shivering, bravely shaking the Christmas morning snow off her pale gray fur, was assisted with gentle licks and soft brushings from the overworked paws of her calico daughter, while the Scratchit kittens, two boys and a girl, came tearing in on little wobbly legs.

"There's Father coming in the cat door with supper," cried two of the young tiger-striped Scratchits. "Let's hide!"

All the Scratchits hid themselves, scurrying into cupboards, sliding behind stacks of mixing bowls, slipping under piles of newly washed aprons, standing still as porcelain pitchers so as not to be seen. And in came Tomcat Scratchit, the father, his sparse tan coat appearing newly brushed to look seasonal, and carrying tiniest Tiny Tomcat by the scruff of his neck.

"Where's our family?"

"Not home!" squealed the smallest one.

"Not home upon Christmas Day!"

The smallest Scratchit, not wanting to see him disappointed, jumped off the shelf prematurely, causing a great soup server to fall with a clang, and ran right up to him, while the two young Scratchits helped Tiny Tomcat, the smallest and frailest of the litter, down to the floor.

"And how did Tiny Tomcat behave?" asked Mother Scratchit.

"Like the perfect kitten," said his father, "and better. He told me coming home that he hoped people noticed he was small and frail, to remind them upon Christmas Day of who it was that loved them all equally, weak and strong, pedigreed or stray."

There never was such a meal as the one Tomcat Scratchit delivered to his family. Despite its small size, the catch was praised for its tenderness and flavor, with everyone having something to say about it, and nobody thinking it was a small fowl for such a large family.

When the dinner was done and all whiskers had been thoroughly licked clean, the family curled around the hearth in a circle, and Tomcat Scratchit proposed:

"A merry Christmas to us all, my dears. God bless us!"

Which the family re-echoed.

"God bless us every one!" said Tiny Tomcat, the last of all.

He snuggled very close to his father's side while his mother licked his tiny brow and nuzzled his weak little body; they both loved the kitten dearly and dreaded that he might be taken from them.

"Spirit," said Scratch, looking on from the sidelines, and now showing an interest he had never felt before, "tell me if Tiny Tomcat will survive."

"If these shadows remain unaltered by the Future," the Ghost replied, "Tiny Tomcat will perish."

"No, no," wailed Scratch. "Say he will be spared!"

*   *   *

It was the last of the three spirits. The Phantom slowly, gravely, silently approached. By the time it drew near him, Scratch was vainly attempting to conceal his shaking body as well as his madly twitching tail behind an oil painting that lay against a cellar wall. The very air through which this Spirit moved seemed to scatter gloom and mystery.

It was shrouded in a deep black fog that concealed its head, its face, its form, leaving nothing visible save for some silvery whiskers and one outstretched paw showing rapier long nails. Its mysterious presence filled him with a solemn dread.

"Am I in the presence of the Ghost of Christmas Yet to Come?" asked Scratch, in a pitiful squeak.

The Apparition answered not, but pointed downward with its paw.

"You are about to show me shadows of things that have not happened but will happen in the time ahead?" Scratch pursued.

Its whiskers appeared to twitch in answer. This was all it said.

"Lead on! Lead on, Spirit! The night is waning fast, and I know you have much to show me and your purpose is to do me good!" Scratch implored.

They scarcely seemed to enter the city; for the city rather seemed to spring up about them. Scratch recognized it as the street by his own house.

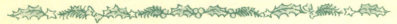

The Spirit stopped beside a group of strays gathered under the window ledge. Observing that the Spirit's paw was pointed at them, Scratch advanced and listened.

"What kind of cat would choose to spend every precious moment of its life fixated upon a mouse hole?" snarled a scrawny gray tabby with the long, pointed face of a rodent.

"Never lived for a minute!" added a Manx missing part of an ear.

"He ignored his family, denied his fellow creatures, never tossed us a tiny morsel, and now, they say, he's dead!"

"A small tin of catnip and a crate of old dish towels is all he left behind," the Manx said.

Crouching low on his haunches, tail between his legs, eyes narrowed in disgust, ears flattened in disgrace, Scratch listened to this dialogue in horror.

"Spirit, I see, I see! The case of this miserable cat might be my own. My life tends that way now. But I am not the cat I once was. Why show me this if I am past all hope?"

The Spirit's whiskers trembled.

"I will honor Christmas in my heart and try to keep it all the year. Assure me that I yet may change these shadows you have shown me by altering my life!"

Holding his paws together in one last prayer to have his fate reversed, he saw a change come over the Phantom. It shrank, collapsed, and dwindled down into the copper pot beside his crate.

*   *   *

Yes! The cellar was once again all his own. His crate was his own. Best and happiest of all, the time before him was his own, to make the most of now.

"I will live in the Past, the Present, and the Future!" Scratch repeated as he crawled out of bed. "All Three Spirits will live within me! Ghost of Snarley, be praised! I am as light as a feather, I am as free as a bird, I am as merry as a kitten! Meow! Merry Christmas to all! Whoop! Meow!"

Frisking up the cellar steps, he ran straightaway to the parlor and, bounding up to an open window, put out his head. No fog. No mist. Clear, bright, golden sunlight; heavenly sky; sweet fresh air; merry bells. Glorious!

"What's today?" he called down to a young male kitten newly brushed and combed.

"Today? Why, it's Christmas Day!" replied the astonished little cat.

"Christmas Day! Thank my whiskers! I haven't missed it!" Scratch said to himself.

"My fine kitten, can your nose direct you to the poultry store around the corner?"

"Yes. Of course!"

"Wonderful kitten! Remarkable cat! Well—you know the prize turkey in the window—the big one?"

"The one as big as me?"

"What a witty kitten. Yes, that one! Bring it back here,

and I'll give you a leg for yourself and a saucer of cream to go with it!"

The kitten was off like a shot.

"I'll send the bird to the Scratchits, but I won't let them know it came from me! Why it's twice the size of Tiny Tomcat!"

While the turkey was being delivered, Ebenezer Scratch, still shaking with excitement, gave himself a thorough bath right down to the last whisker, cleaned his ears, trimmed his nails, combed his fur to its Sunday best, and at last got out into the streets.

From every direction, creatures poured forth, and Scratch regarded every one of them with a delighted look, and to each he offered a roaring purr. He looked so irresistibly friendly that three or four good-humored felines said, "Good morning! A merry Christmas to you!" And Scratch said often afterward that, of all the sweet sounds he had ever heard, those were the sweetest in his ears.

He had not gone far, when coming toward him, over the cobblestones, he beheld the rodent-faced stray and his Manx friend.

"My dear cats," said Scratch, quickening his pace and moving within a nose's length of the two old felines, "a merry Christmas to you both!"

"Mr. Scratch?"

"Yes," said Scratch. "That is my name, and it is a name the

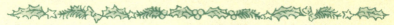

poultry shop is well familiar with. Please do me the honor of visiting this very same poultry shop, as my guests! I will see that you, and as many strays as you can round up, are well provided with a fine Christmas feast!"

"But, sir! We don't know how to thank ..."

"Don't say anything, please!" retorted Scratch. "And please come and visit me!"

In the afternoon he turned his steps toward his home, and finally, summoning up the courage, he stepped into the pantry, where the Scratchit family was fully assembled.

"Why, bless my soul, who's that?"

"It's I, your Uncle Scratch," he growled in his accustomed voice, as near as he could feign it. "What's this! Engaging in merriment and gobbling up turkey when you should be attending to your mouse holes?"

Seeing the fur on their little backs rise up in fright, Scratch began to laugh: a big, jolly, warm laugh, which was followed by an even jollier purr, as the treats and gifts he had collected for each cat spilled out all over the pantry floor.

"A merry Christmas, Tomcat and Mother Scratchit, all you lovely Scratchit cats and kittens, and for you, Tiny Tomcat, a special kiss on the head. I have come to visit," he continued. "Will you have me?"

Sensing the extraordinary change in him, and rejoicing at this great outpouring of warmth, the Scratchits chose to embrace their uncle; curling around him, nuzzling his face and

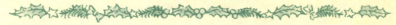

ears, licking his fur, proffering soft looks and gentle conversation; making him feel more content than he'd ever felt in his life, and for the first time, completely at home.

Scratch was better than his word. He did all he said he would, and more. He became as good a feline as the good old world has ever known, and to Tiny Tomcat, who did not perish, he became a second father.

It was always said of him that he knew how to keep Christmas well. May that be said of us all! And so, as Tiny Tomcat observed, God Bless Us, Every One!

A Cat's Christmas Prayer

Whoever made the stars that shine,
Whoever made green trees of pine,
Whoever dreamed up fish and mice,
Or sun and rain and snow and ice,
Must have the power in His paws
To help when there's a worthy cause.
Whoever gave the birds a nest
Will grant this humble cat's request.

For needy felines everywhere,
I meow my little Christmas prayer.
Please heal the sick
And cheer the sad,
Forgive the naughty,
And excuse the bad.

One more simple thing I ask:
A pool of sunlight in which to bask,
Plus a plate of food,
A safe, warm house,
A loving lap, and a catnip mouse.
Freedom from fleas, furballs, and mats,
And homes for all the homeless cats.

A Cat's Christmas Journal

A Place for Pussycats to Record Their Special Memories

My Most Entertaining Holiday Moments:

While trimming the tree:

While wrapping presents:

While entertaining:

While feasting:

Gifts Caught:

Gifts Received:

Gifts Devoured:

Gifts Stashed under the Bed:

My Favorite Christmas Scent:

My Favorite Christmas Meal:

My Favorite Christmas Present:

Next Year's List for Santa Paws:

-

-

-

-

-

-